National Incomes Policy
for Inflation Control

by

Charles E. Rockwood

FLORIDA STATE UNIVERSITY PRESS
Tallahassee 1969

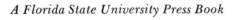

A Florida State University Press Book

To the memory of
GEORGE HERBERT ROCKWOOD, JR.
PROFESSOR OF ELECTRICAL ENGINEERING
UNIVERSITY OF ILLINOIS

PREFACE

THEORIES OF INFLATION that emphasize the causative role of wages
have been popular in the literature of economics for nearly twenty
years. The wage inflation idea still is controversial, but its adher-
ents are numerous and often prominent.

Despite this popularity, economists have not devoted adequate
attention to the study of policy remedies which flow from the wage
inflation idea. This is especially the case for the material treated in
this book. Direct controls on wages are perhaps the most obvious
policy implication of a wage-price theory. But, in spite of the obvi-
ousness of the policy suggestion, no general treatise on national
incomes policy as an anti wage-inflation device appears to exist,
and, predictably, policy makers have been disinclined to wait until
one appears. A majority of nations in the world already have instituted a system of direct controls on wages with at least some
anti-inflation intent, if not result. Even the United States, with
its "Guideposts to Non-Inflationary Wage Bargaining," has not
been immune to the trend. In practice, obviously, these are wage
controls informally applied.

It is therefore the intent of this volume to provide a general
analysis of the value of a national incomes policy for inflation
control. To the extent that the objective is accomplished it is
partly the result of those who took an interest in the work and made
some contribution to it.

The assistance of Professor Henry M. Oliver, Jr., of Indiana

University and Professor Persis R. Emmett, now Persis Rockwood, of The Florida State University is particularly to be appreciated. The debt of scholarship, be it good or bad, is enormous, certainly. But of those who influenced the content and direction of this work in an important way, the contribution of these two stands out from among the others.

For the help of Professors Henry Oliver, Persis Emmett Rockwood, and others, I am truly grateful.

CHARLES E. ROCKWOOD

Tallahassee
June, 1968

TABLE OF CONTENTS

Chapter 1

INTRODUCTION

Recent efforts at inflation control in the United States and elsewhere have included attempts to limit general wage increases by governmental fiat. Such an approach is predicated upon the assumption that price level stability and full employment would not otherwise be completely compatible objectives. A frequent contention is that "too high" wage rates moving upward "too quickly" are the chief reason for this partial incompatibility. The belief is that restrictive monetary and fiscal policy measures sufficient to halt upward price-level movements result in "excessive" unemployment.

Acceptance of a wage inflation hypothesis of this sort underlies a variety of policy proposals for inflation control. Prominent among them, of course, is direct control of wages. Many who accept some form of wage inflation thesis contend that governmentally established limits to private bargaining over wages are either necessary or useful as an anti-inflationary device. This is the proposition that will be examined. More specifically, the analysis will center upon the efficacy of a national incomes policy for inflation control when used in conjunction with price stabilizing monetary and fiscal policy.

In the evaluation of the pros and cons of national incomes policy as an anti-inflationary device, an essential question is—incomes policy of what sort? What regulatory and administrative criteria should be used? What are the relative advantages (disad-

1

vantages) of each? A number of approaches might be selected for the analysis. This study elects to concentrate greatest effort on an incomes policy to combat wage inflation where it is assumed that the classic case of demand-pull inflation also may be a problem. Such a control program is presumed to consist of a two-pronged approach to the inflation problem. As an attack upon demand inflation when it occurs, price stabilizing monetary and fiscal policy would be used. This, in itself, is a controversial part of the control program. It will require examination. But the examination will not be in detail for that is not the central task of this work. As an attack upon wage inflation, which is considered to be a chronic problem, direct controls upon wages would be used. The major task of this book will be to examine this aspect of the control program, but the examination involves analysis of ideas and concepts not specifically a part of such a program.

The wage-push theory which underlies this sort of control program is controversial. This book does not try to judge its validity. The central question is: If this wage-push inflation theory is valid, what "suitable" criteria can be developed and employed for administering national incomes policy as a complement to price stabilizing monetary and fiscal policy?

A closely related second question is: If this wage-push theory is not valid, can an anti-inflation program, administered in accordance with the above criteria, ease the task of price-stabilizing monetary and fiscal policy by checking the pressure on the authorities for expansionary policies—and, if this is so, can the program be pushed without the creation of evils as bad or worse than those which they replace?

The requirements of a suitable program are several: (1) It must not hinder monetary and fiscal policy aimed at keeping aggregate monetary demand at that level which would maintain "full" employment plus price-level stability in the absence of wage-push inflation forces. If possible, it should reinforce monetary and fiscal policy aimed at price-level stability. (2) It must not "distort" the allocation of resources or the distribution of income. (3) It must not so alter incentives and attitudes as drastically to affect the nature of the economic system. Or, rather, in the case of the latter two requirements, the program must not produce these evils to a greater extent than that combination of unemployment and/or inflation which is believed to be the alternative to the program.

Concern is not, therefore, with a Netherlands type program where the chief policy tool for inflation control is wage rate regulation alone and where excess demand and hence repressed inflation frequently exist. Nor is concern with a short-period, wage control program such as that experienced in the United States and many other countries during World War II. Rather, interest is in a permanent control program, the essential task of which is to suggest the wage level appropriate in a particular situation and the contingent wage pattern.

It is, therefore, perhaps even somewhat misleading to imply that this study is concerned with appraisal of the effectiveness of a wage control program in combatting inflation, because more is intended. Certainly it is important to know what wage program seems most likely to facilitate achievement of price-level stability by moderating the level (structure too perhaps) of wages so as to ease management of monetary and fiscal policy. But it may be even more important to know whether a national incomes policy, properly structured, can eliminate the adverse side effects of unemployment and output decline sometimes associated with unequivocal pursuit of price-level stability. And, if this can be aided by some sort of wage control program, what would be the "costs" of the policy.

The requirements of such a program for wage controls raise a variety of definitional questions: What is meant by "price-level stability?" By "full employment?" By "distortion of patterns of resource allocation" or of "income distribution?" And, by "altering the basic nature of the economic system?"

Closely related to these questions are certain others: Why is price-level stability desired? Is this the only concept of inflation for which concern need be evidenced? What evils are believed to be associated with price-level increases? With what durations and intensities of price-level increases are these evils presumed to be connected? Why is full employment desired? What evils are believed to be associated with what durations and intensities of unemployment?

This book will not discuss these definitional and closely related questions extensively. But, because judgments which the main questions require depend upon answers given to these secondary questions, Part I briefly discusses why full employment and price-level stability are desired.

Part II, which begins with Chapter 5, asks the central question: If the wage-push theory of inflation is valid, what suitable criteria can be developed and employed for administering a national incomes policy as a complement to price-stabilizing monetary and fiscal arrangements?

Part II thus represents the core of the work. It is this section which develops some basic principles for national incomes policy as an anti-inflationary device and some general observations about the efficiency of the policy that is developed. Part III is an addition to this foundation.

Part III investigates the second major question: If the wage-push theory of inflation is not valid, can an anti wage-push control program ease the task of price stabilizing monetary and fiscal policy by checking the pressure on the authorities for expansionary policies? If so, can the program be implemented without the creation of evils as much or more disliked than the ones they replace?

Part III draws heavily upon the analysis of Part II. Essentially Part III is a survey of the ways in which conclusions reached in Part II would need to be amended if the inflation experienced were not of the wage-push type. No attempt is made at complete and exhaustive analysis of problems which would be raised if this inflation theory were incorrect but the wage control proposal were implemented.

In summary, this book deals with the efficacy of national incomes policy as a companion to price stabilizing monetary and fiscal policy for inflation control. This is a broad question. It cuts across many subjects and involves many unsettled issues. To facilitate analysis the study is limited sharply in scope. The work is primarily theoretical in character as no serious attempt is made to test empirically the many issues discussed. Further, most of the numerous related legal, sociological and political questions are excluded, as are issues of economic welfare analysis.

As mentioned earlier, the study seeks to avoid direct entry into the inflation controversy by considering, in turn, a variety of inflation theories as underlying a program for limiting the freedom which private parties have in bargaining over wages. The analysis concentrates upon testing the idea of wage controls to combat wage inflation. But application of the developed wage guides in other situations also is treated, although not so elaborately. This procedure enables avoidance of the difficult issue of inflation cause.

But, indirectly it ultimately has a bearing on that issue. The usefulness of national incomes policy for inflation control, both in wage inflation situations and in non-wage inflation situations, is relevant to the question of inflation cause.

If, for example, the developed program were unsatisfactory regardless of the cause of inflation, this would diminish the importance of the wage-push inflation theory. It would rule out one policy conclusion to which the wage-push theory leads. Or, if an incomes policy would work equally well to limit price-level inflation regardless of the inflation cause, the importance of distinctions between theories of cause would be diminished. One proposal, national incomes policy, would not depend upon cause. Or again, if a national incomes policy has an excellent chance of controlling at least one cause of inflation, this well might encourage experimentation with controls in the hope that future inflationary pressures would be controllable varieties.

As a final point, the analysis is time dated, not only in the usual sense that theories may change or knowledge may change, but also in the sense that the observed incompatibility between full employment and price-level stability may disappear, if indeed it ever existed. If this incompatibility should disappear, so would the problem which the study treats. It might seem that this qualification is no more than a caution that the world may change over time, and so it is. But, it is also more than this.

Continued pursuance of the goal of full employment without sufficient regard to the "costs" of a guarantee of "adequate" employment opportunities may have caused an "inflationary bias" in our economy. If a policy of price-level stability were pursued ruthlessly for a considerable period of time it might cause the disappearance of the observed inflationary bias. Thus, the prediction here is not that the world may change, but that a specified change is possible.

PART I

Theories of the Cause and Impact of Inflation

Chapter 2

EMPLOYMENT AND INFLATION

Adequate discussion of inflation cause (the purpose of the following chapter) and impact (the purpose of Chapter 4) is not possible without some understanding of the term "inflation" and the concept of full employment as each relates to inflation theory. Some definition of inflation and of full employment (unemployment) is inherent in any discussion of inflation cause. Some assumptions as to cause are inherent in any discussion of impact. Further, seemingly conflicting theories of cause or impact may not involve theoretical disagreement at all, but only different definitions of full employment. In other words, the degree of compatibility between full employment and economic stability in a given instance depends upon the meaning of stability selected, the definition of full employment used, and the cause or causes of existing unemployment.

The purpose of this chapter is briefly to define inflation and then to examine the role of employment objectives and causes of unemployment in an analysis of inflation. The discussion is relevant both to the issue of inflation cause and to that of inflation impact. In the course of the discussion in this chapter and the two that follow, it should become increasingly evident that, given a definition of inflation: (1) often there is a close relationship between theories as to causes of unemployment and theories of inflation; and (2) selected social goals are quite apt to color employment and stabilization objectives.

7

CONCEPT OF INFLATION

This book is concerned with the control of price-level inflation. Price-level inflation is defined here as the upward movement
of final product prices. This is not the only type of inflation which
might be selected for control. It is, however, the type most commonly singled out for consideration and is selected for that reason.

It would be possible to discuss wage controls as an anti-inflationary device and mean by inflation something other than price-
level inflation. But it would not be possible to substitute another
definition of inflation for price-level inflation and leave the analysis
of this work unaffected. Inflation differently defined would have a
different impact and would require different control techniques.

Unfortunately, definition of inflation as price-level inflation
does not give a clear indication of the type of inflation with which
this study must deal. This is because price-level inflations can be
of differing natures and differing causes. Classified according to outward manifestations of their character or by reactions of individuals
to their character, price-level inflations may be: anticipated or unanticipated, mild or rapid, broken trend or unbroken trend, open
or repressed. Classified according to cause, price-level inflations
may be: demand-pull, cost-push, or of the Schultze structuralist type.

This book does not attempt to limit consideration to any one
type of price-level inflation. Instead an effort is made to consider
many possible forms which the inflation might take. This adds
greatly to the complexity of the analysis. It is to be hoped that it
adds also to its value.

CONCEPTS OF FULL EMPLOYMENT

As a second definitional problem, there are a multitude of
possible concepts of full employment and, therefore, of unemployment. Each definition, if selected as a policy goal, has associated price-level implications. In an effort to demonstrate this
relationship, there will be outlined here representative definitions
of full employment which have been proposed as policy goals
together with the type(s) of price-level pressures, if any, that
would be generated in each case, if the goals were pursued. As will
be seen these definitions are formulated, at least in part, on the

basis of an assumption as to the cause(s) of unemployment. For it is not possible to reach conclusions about the inflationary impact of efforts to pursue certain employment goals until the policy measures that will be used are known, and until the kind of unemployment assumed is known.

Matters of inflation cause somewhat aside for the moment, the prime object of a working definition of full employment should be to delimit frictional unemployment, including both seasonal and structural unemployment. Viewed from this standpoint, the common definition of full employment, "jobs for all who are willing and able to work," is rather inadequate. It seems to ignore the existence of frictional unemployment, although the matter does depend somewhat upon how such terms as "willing," "able," and "jobs" are defined, not a simple task under the best of circumstances.[1]

The definition of jobs for all who are willing and able to work, however, may be altered slightly to become a policy goal that is reasonably clear. For example, full employment could be defined as job openings in numbers at least equal to the number of unemployed. This was the Beveridge goal of full employment.[2] It was approximately equivalent, from the standpoint of effect on aggregate demand, to what Ohlin termed over-full employment.[3]

Of course some frictional unemployment always will exist. Therefore, creation of jobs in numbers at least equal to the number of applicants who are in some sense qualified would be inflationary. Within the Beveridge framework this was considered tolerable for two reasons: first, because full employment was regarded as so important a social goal;[4] second, because according to Lord Beveridge the exigencies of that excess demand needed to generate his full employment could be controlled easily.[5]

When Beveridge advocated his definition of full employment as a policy goal, he recognized both that his would conflict with

1. For a summary treatment of some of the definitional problems that are encountered here see Henry M. Oliver, Jr., *A Critique of Socioeconomic Goals* (Bloomington: Indiana University Press, 1954), pp. 131-39.

2. Lord William Beveridge, *Full Employment in a Free Society* (London: George Allen and Unwin, Ltd., 1944), pp. 18-20.

3. Bertil Ohlin, *The Problem of Employment Stabilization* (New York: Columbia University Press, 1949), p. 6.

4. *Full Employment in a Free Society*, p. 19.

5. *Ibid.*, pp. 198-203.

customary definitions of full employment,[6] and that it involved
the generation of upward price-level pressures. Beveridge type
full employment would not be compatible with price-level stability.
In fact Beveridge showed great concern over the possibility of
inflation. This was evidenced by his suggestion that direct controls
might be a necessary corollary to his plan.[7]

Less ambitious employment goals than the Beveridge one
would yield less intense inflationary pressures. Conceivably, a deflationary goal might even be selected, although probably only as
a consequence of policy error. That is, policy makers presumably
would set such a conservative goal only when they did not realize
their target level of employment was less than would occur with
price-level stability.

As an entirely different method of defining a national employment goal from that used by Beveridge, full employment might be
defined in a circular manner. Instead of defining full employment
quantitively, it would be defined as whatever level of employment
resulted from specified policy actions. In a sense, full employment
would be defined as the derivative of a "proper" economic environment. Price-level implications of this type of objective would
depend upon the meaning of a proper economic environment.

The definition of full employment to which A. C. Pigou adhered is one example of a circular definition. According to Pigou,
full employment was that level of employment which was obtained,
or would be obtained quickly, under reasonably competitive conditions.[8] In the absence of extreme and continuing exogenous
changes[9] which would prevent the approximation of a state of
equilibrium in the real world, any unemployment that persisted
would be considered voluntary. Under the Pigou definition no
attempt should be made to adjust the level of unemployment that
is voluntary in this sense, because that would interfere with free
choice. This definition of full employment implies cyclical price-
level changes that fluctuate about a constant value.

Another way in which full employment could be defined circularly would be to say that full employment is whatever level of

6. *Ibid.*, p. 18.
7. *Ibid.*, pp. 202-03.
8. *Employment and Equilibrium* (London: Macmillan and Co., Ltd.,
1941), pp. 77-91.
9. An example would be large and inappropriate changes in the supply
of money.

employment is compatible with stable prices and reasonable growth potential. This is illustrated by the Mints position.[10]

Any unemployment, according to Mints, which occurred in a situation of stable prices (a concept which itself calls for rigorous definition) occurred in spite of sound monetary management, and was probably either frictional or voluntary in nature, but in any case such unemployment was non-monetary in origin. In the Mints view no attempt should be made to correct the essentially non-monetary aberration by monetary means.

The Mints analysis flows from a belief that a policy of price-level stabilization, firmly adhered to, over time will result in the highest possible level of employment. For this reason Mints will be discussed in the section on causes of unemployment as well. It is also true, however, that Mints likely would have continued to hold the view that price-level stability should override attainment of the highest possible level of employment as the paramount economic goal even if he believed that higher levels of employment could be obtained and maintained only at the expense of price-level stability. For Mints full employment clearly was associated with price stability.

In between the two extremes of full employment defined as jobs for all and full employment defined as whatever employment the economy experiences when appropriate policies are pursued, lies a host of attempts at pinpointing an acceptable level of unemployment.[11] What would be acceptable would depend upon a number of factors including: (1) the institutional setting, (2) the relative importance attached to measurable employment objectives,[12] and (3) the comparative difficulty of attaining various levels of employment. Each objective, definition, has its own price-level implications.

10. Lloyd W. Mints, *Monetary Policy for a Competitive Society* (New York: McGraw-Hill, 1950), pp. 27-28.

11. For representative definitions of a contrasting sort (in addition to those already cited) see Joan Robinson, "Disguised Unemployment," *Economic Journal*, June, 1936, pp. 225-37 [this article has been reprinted with some changes in her book, *Essays in the Theory of Employment* (Oxford: Basil Blackwell, 1953), pp. 60-74]; J. M. Keynes, *The General Theory of Employment, Interest, and Money* (New York: Harcourt, Brace and Company, 1936), pp. 4-18; and Bertil Ohlin, *The Problem of Employment Stabilization*, pp. 3-26.

12. The problems involved in selecting a measurable concept of full employment, and the pitfalls to be aware of when doing so, have been the subject of a great number of journal articles, e.g., Clarence Long, "The Concept of

CAUSES OF UNEMPLOYMENT

The cause of unemployment, assumed or actual, is another important determinant of the compatibility of full employment and stable prices. The cause of unemployment, other things remaining equal, affects the type and rate of inflation. More intense corrective efforts are required to eliminate unemployment of some types than others. The cause of unemployment and, therefore, the relative difficulty of its elimination, also may affect the degree of perfection which is written into the policy definition of full employment.

This section is concerned with two issues: What are the general causes of unemployment which have received prominent mention? What is the inflationary impact, if any, of eliminating different types of unemployment through use of monetary and fiscal policy to maintain aggregate demand at "appropriate" levels?

Keynesian Unemployment. One of the more familiar types of unemployment described in economic literature is that said to result from a general deficiency in aggregate demand, a "deficiency" that may be permanent or self-correcting. This is the conception of unemployment so often associated with J. M. Keynes.

Specific reference is to the now traditional Keynesian diagonal cross analysis. In other words, begin with an assumed marginal propensity to consume of less than unity, and plans to invest such that at times the equilibrium level of output and employment would be less than capacity. Under these conditions the aggregate supply function for an advanced Western economy then might be expected to be such that a substantial rise in the level of employment could be achieved at the expense of a slight increase in average price levels. Most of the time this is a level of employment which the economy eventually would reach anyway. Through ap-

---

Unemployment," *Quarterly Journal of Economics,* November, 1942, pp. 1-31; Thomas K. Hitch, "Meaning and Measurement of 'Full' or 'Maximum' Employment," *Review of Economics and Statistics,* February, 1951, pp. 1-12; Robert S. Weinberg, "Full Employment 1955-60—A Feasibility Test," *American Economic Review,* December, 1953, pp. 860-64; Stanley Lebergott, "Measuring Unemployment," *Review of Economics and Statistics,* November, 1954, pp. 390-401; Edwin G. Nourse, "Ideal and Working Concepts of Full Employment," *American Economic Review,* May, 1957, pp. 97-115. The point of view of a political scientist, rather than that of an economist, may be appraised in Stephen K. Bailey, "Political Elements in Full Employment Policy," *American Economic Review,* May, 1955, pp. 341-51.

propriate monetary and fiscal policy action, the objective is assured, and the time period of adjustment can be shortened considerably. The unfortunate cost, of course, is that the measures which help to stimulate employment also are likely to bring about inflation—a policy conclusion that Patinkin shows can follow from a revised and updated version of the quantity theory of money as well as from the Keynesian theories.[13]

Opposition to the concept of a necessary policy choice between inflation and high employment may appear to represent a challenge to the Keynesian belief in a relatively elastic aggregate supply function up to the point of full employment. Indeed this could be what is intended. That is, the contention might be that at any given point in time the aggregate supply curve for the economy begins to slope upward measurably, before even near-full employment is reached. In this case rapid, not mild, inflation would be associated with attempts to remove or reduce unemployment of the Keynesian type, but this still would be inflation of the stair-step variety.

On the other hand it could be that those who indicate a desire to challenge the Keynesian conception of a relatively elastic supply function really are challenging the Keynesian definition of full employment. Then price-level implications would depend upon the definition that was substituted. Specifically, some of the challengers to the Keynesian analysis seem to argue not that Keynes was incorrect in his evaluation of the nature of the aggregate supply function, but that: (1) Keynes was too liberal in his definition of full employment (i.e., he tolerated too high a level of frictional unemployment), and (2) although his appraisal of the costs of reaching his employment goal were substantially correct, the analysis is not relevant, because the costs of reaching some other employment goal are not the same.

There is a difference between the analysis that leads to an evaluation of the intensity of the cost, in terms of degree of price-level change, that will result when appropriate monetary and fiscal policy is employed to enable achievement of full employment in the Keynesian sense and an analysis of the relative costs of achieving a more ambitious employment objective.

In the first instance the discussion is in terms of a comparative

13. Don Patinkin, *Money, Interest, and Prices* (Evanston: Row Peterson, and Co., 1956).

statics type of analysis, where the economy moves from a position of less than full employment to one of full employment. The Keynesian framework is a useful analytical tool in this case. In the second instance the discussion is in terms of a moving equilibrium where an aggregate supply curve of the Keynesian type would be continually shifting rightward and upward. Here the Keynesian framework is cumbersome.

It seems likely that in this latter situation it would be wisest to drop the reference to aggregate supply curves and talk of how, by taking advantage of lags, money illusion, etc., frictional unemployment might be reduced at the cost of trend increases in the price-level. This amounts to stating that an examination of the shape of the aggregate supply curve facing a given economy at a given point in time does not help in the development of the "science" of perpetuating a Beveridge type situation of over-full employment, nor in an appraisal of the costs in terms of price-level change of doing same.[14]

Schultze and Slichter Unemployment. The above leads rather directly into a further analysis of the causes of frictional unemployment and an analysis of means by which this element may be reduced in magnitude. In this respect the views of Charles L. Schultze[15] and Sumner Slichter[16] contain revealing insights that bear on the issue of inflation and its control.

Professor Schultze contends that, because of certain institutional barriers that hinder price flexibility, shifts in demand, which are going on all the time, will not be offset perfectly by supply shifts. This means one of two policy alternatives, unemployment or mild trend inflation. This conclusion also is akin to the Slichter position that mild inflation facilitates the flow of resources

14. Analysis of this sort of trade-off has been the subject of a large body of literature arising out of the pioneer work by A. W. Phillips, "The Relation Between Unemployment and the Rate of Change of Money Wage Rates in the United Kingdom, 1861-1957," *Economica,* November, 1958, pp. 283-99. Perhaps the best known of this body of literature is Richard G. Lipsey, "The Relation Between Unemployment and the Rate of Change of Money Wage Rates in the United Kingdom, 1862-1957: A Further Analysis," *Economica,* February, 1960, pp. 1-31.

15. *Recent Inflation in the United States,* study paper No. 1, prepared in connection with the study of employment, growth and price levels, U. S. Congress, Joint Economic Committee, 85th Cong., 1st Sess., 1959.

16. See, for example, U. S. Congress, Joint Economic Committee, *Hearings,* Part I—*The American Economy: Problems and Prospects,* March 20, 23, 24, and 25, 1959 (Washington: U. S. Government Printing Office, 1959), pp. 2-53.

and thereby stimulates output and employment. The primary difference between the two is that under the Slichter argument money illusion played an important role. It is not essential to the Schultze explanation.

Within the framework of both the Schultze and the Slichter arguments, mild inflation can result in higher levels of employment. It helps offset certain structural inadequacies that hinder the mobility of factors of production.

Mints Type Unemployment. A rather different point of view from that of Schultze and Slichter is evidenced by the Mints position. As noted earlier,[17] according to Mints the appropriate employment goal was that level of employment which is compatible with price-level stability.

More than this, Mints argued that although structural unemployment might be reduced temporarily by inflating aggregate demand at the expense of price-level stability, this would result in a lower secular level of employment than otherwise would occur. Mints' primary argument was that inflation caused unemployment through introduction of an increase in business uncertainty.[18] But, he also expressed the belief that inflations have a tendency to foster unsustainable booms,[19] a position similar to one Fellner takes.[20] Mints believed that irresponsible monetary management results in the introduction of additional wage rigidities which hamper the functioning of a free economy.[21]

The Mints argument closely parallels that portion of Chapter 4 where the possibility is considered that inflation has a depressing influence on output and employment. It is in accord with the Keynesian thought that employment levels may be raised by increases in the supply of money. It disagrees with Keynes, and even more emphatically with the Slichter type approach, that inflationary increases in aggregate monetary demand are judicious policy. Mints contends that resulting increases in employment levels would be temporary only and more than offset by later employment declines.

Lerner High Full and Low Full Employment. Another concept of the cause of unemployment is involved in Abba Lerner's high

17. *Supra*, pp. 10-11.
18. *Monetary Policy for a Competitive Society*, p. 13.
19. *Ibid.*, p. 11.
20. William Fellner, *Trends and Cycles in Economic Activity* (New York: Henry Holt, 1956).
21. *Monetary Policy for a Competitive Society*, p. 27.

and low full employment.[22] These two definitions were formulated by Lerner as a result of his belief that the bargaining power of labor is excessive and of his belief in the prevalence of downward wage rigidities.

Lerner speaks, then, of two employment positions. The lower is that level of employment which is compatible with price stability. This would be the Mints full employment position. The upper is more nearly akin to that level of employment which Slichter was striving to attain.

The interesting distinction between Lerner and Slichter is that Lerner agrees with the Mints position. Lerner believes high full employment cannot be maintained, continuously, through inflationary finance. But, in contrast to what Mints would suggest, Lerner seeks to obtain the high full employment position anyway. For Lerner, this is to be accomplished through direct controls on the labor sector of the economy.

CONCLUSION

A definition of full employment is at least implicit in any theory of inflation cause and impact. Differences in the definition of full employment, for example, have a great deal to do with the differences between Mints and Slichter as to the cause of inflation.

The cause of unemployment also has a bearing on the relative difficulty of its elimination. Treatment of cyclical or seasonal unemployment thus may be quite different from the treatment of structural unemployment. Differing cyclical, seasonal, or structural unemployment experiences often will call for different policy remedies. Because of this, the selected policy definition of full employment well may vary, depending upon the relative difficulty (assumed or actual) of eliminating the particular inflationary experience with which the policy maker must deal.

22. *Economics of Employment* (New York: McGraw-Hill Book Company, Inc., 1951), pp. 17-30.

Chapter 3

CAUSES OF INFLATION

A MAJOR PREMISE of this study is that there are advantages to evaluating one often suggested inflation palliative, national incomes policy, in light of each of several possible theories of cause. With this described purpose, the importance of analysis and discussion of hypotheses about price-level inflation cause is obvious. However, any analysis of cause would be incomplete without an understanding of the relationship which exists between theories of cause and type of unemployment assumed, or definition of full employment adopted. Thus there is an especially close tie between this chapter and the discussion of employment concepts and inflation in Chapter 2.

HYPOTHESIZED CAUSES OF INFLATION

There is more than one way to categorize theories of inflation cause. Under certain assumptions, and for certain types of price-level inflation, analysis of the aggregate supply curve may be of help in determining the compatibility or incompatibility of stable price-levels and full employment, or at least in illustrating the relationship between inflation and certain other economic variables.[1] However, inflation is a dynamic phenomenon and in attempting to analyze it in what are essentially static terms (e.g., the Keynesian type aggregate supply curve) it is possible to become immersed in

1. *Supra*, Chapter 12.

theoretical conundrums which could be avoided by abandoning the approach.

Thus, a situation of continuing price-level inflation could be explained in terms of the usual aggregate supply and demand functions. But this implies shifts in both the aggregate supply and the aggregate demand curves. The question then would become, what occasioned the shifts? Specifically, it must be assumed that one of the two curves shifted first and the other shift was induced.

A shift in aggregate demand, for example, initially would result in a movement up the aggregate supply curve. Prices would rise somewhat. Because prices for one are costs for another, the basic data upon which the original aggregate supply curve was constructed would have changed. A new higher curve would have to be constructed. This process presumably would be repeated until a new equilibrium was reached at which output reverted to the old level, but the price-level was higher than before.

Clearly a model of this sort is very crude. For example, no real balance effect is incorporated. But the model does underscore an important economic relationship. Thus, the aggregate supply and demand type analysis can be used to focus attention on the crucial question of shifts in the curve, albeit in a somewhat awkward manner. But it does not explain adequately what caused the shifting process to begin, nor does it explain magnitudes.

Some of these objections can be overcome by reverting to the "new theories of inflation" that have become so much an accepted part of the literature of the post-1950 era. Popularly referred to as demand-pull and cost-push, or more accurately the demand-pull hypothesis and the various rebuttals to it, these basic concepts actually are not all that new. Keynes, in his *Treatise on Money*, talked of spontaneous and induced inflation as early as 1930.[2] Induced inflation, as Keynes defined it, referred to the case where excess demand forced a price rise, and would be equivalent to what is now called demand-pull inflation. Spontaneous inflation, in the Keynesian analysis, referred to inflation which occurred in the absence of excess demand, and would be equivalent to what now is termed cost-push inflation. By whatever terminology, however, the cost-push, demand-pull dichotomy does provide a useful analytical framework, and it is followed in this work for that reason.

2. J. M. Keynes, *A Treatise on Money*, Vol. I: *The Pure Theory of Money* (London: Macmillan and Co., Ltd., 1930), pp. 166-70.

It should be clearly understood, however, that the theories of inflation cause to be considered in this context are theories of predominant cause or most significant cause, in the sense that the variables discussed are politically and economically independent and thus would be amenable to change or influence through governmental action. Because of this, theories discussed may differ in detail or in stipulation of the "chief" causal factor, yet each may be correct in that it suggests a causal factor for a particular inflationary experience. Alternatively, the types of price-level inflation for which causes are suggested may differ. For this reason also, it may be possible to reconcile many of the non-identical theories as to inflation cause.

Demand-Pull Inflation. A positive statement of the demand-pull thesis is not difficult to present, as it is quite straightforward.

Basically the theory assumes that prices function reasonably well as a rationing device so that in-the-main surpluses or shortages are rectified by price changes that clear the market. Given this kind of price behavior, inflation results from an excess of aggregate monetary demand. A shortage of goods is created and prices rise.

Proponents of the demand inflation idea are both numerous and prominent. By and large, support of the demand inflation idea seems to go hand in hand with the contention that heretofore the stabilizing power of sound monetary policy has been underestimated. This contention is associated with the "Chicago School" and advocates of the quantity theory of money generally, but numerous economists who would not accept the views of the "Chicago School" in other matters also adhere to the demand-pull argument.

Typically the demand-pull thesis and contemporary versions of the quantity theory of money argue that optimum levels and patterns of output and employment may result from counter-cyclical monetary (and fiscal) policy, but only when such policy is judiciously applied. Whether the emphasis is upon income and expenditure flows or upon money stocks, trend increases in aggregate monetary demand ought to be commensurate with trend increases in output, and no more.

In other words, most often involved in the demand-pull theory is the presumption that stable price-levels will yield optimum levels of output and employment, or that the goal of price-level stability is paramount, or perhaps both. It is possible to accept the demand-pull thesis and still favor inflationary finance, but this point of view is an unusual one. Should this be the position taken, the argument would have to be that because of lags, money illusion, or some similar explanation, inflation stimulated a higher level of output, employment, and growth and was desirable for that reason.

Obviously the idea that inflation might stimulate output is a point of view that is particularly difficult to accept just now for the United States, because of the balance of payments implications which such a price-level policy would carry. Moreover, it is a point of view that borders on the patently absurd in application to most of the open economies of the world. But this is just to say that under the exchange rate systems popularly in use in the world today it is difficult or impossible, depending upon the national situation, to follow an independent domestic macroeconomic policy. And, it is, of course, out of this dilemma that most of the support for a freely fluctuating exchange rate system derives.

If, instead of the assumption that inflation stimulates the economy, a more usual position is taken and it is concluded that price-level stability should be the policy goal even at the possible sacrifice of employment objectives, the national employment goal has been defined circularly. Neither balance of payments problems nor cost inflation theories need complicate the analysis. Full employment is defined as the level of employment compatible with price-level stability.

As a final possibility, if it is argued that stable price-levels yield the highest possible level of employment, then the demand-pull thesis might be compatible with any of the employment objectives mentioned in the preceding chapter. However, which employment goal was achieved would be a matter of chance rather than design. The level of employment would be the dependent rather than the independent variable in the analysis.

Cost-Push Inflation. Strong opposition to the demand-pull analysis comes from theorists who argue that some inflationary pressures originate not so much from demand as from cost increases. However, in contrast to the demand-pull thesis, where there is only one fairly unified theory to analyze, there are almost as many cost inflation theories as writers on the subject. Cost-push is a collective term.

In its elementary and basic form the cost inflation thesis suggests that costs (prices) rise with or without a preceding or coincidental shift in aggregate demand. If pressure on prices from forces of the demand-pull type exceeds in magnitude similar pressure of the cost-push type, the amount of demand-pull usually is considered the controlling factor in determining price-level changes. If the cost-push force is greater it usually is thought to be controlling. Cost-push theory attempts to explain only one variety of inflation. Because it probably is inoperative as an influencing force if demand-pull is more intense, cost-push usually is accepted as a variety that manifests itself at some times and not at others— a point which should not be interpreted as being inconsistent with the possibility that demand-pull would exist in some markets while cost-push was present in others, what Gardner Ackley refers to as mixed demand-cost inflation.[3]

Suppose now that aggregate supply shifts and supply price rises as a consequence. Let supply price rise to the point where a position of substantially less than full employment is attained. When this happens, according to the cost-push theorists, the government (*i.e.*, the Treasury and/or the Federal Reserve) is forced to step in and bolster effective demand because of the overriding importance of maintaining high employment levels, an explanation for past Federal government actions.

An alternative explanation for past governmental intervention would be that major segments of the economy, government, business and labor, all are competing for an enlarged share of total output, and the competitive method employed by the government is an unbalanced budget. In this case it would merely be fortuitous that the government behaved as it did insofar as the avoidance of unemployment was concerned.

In any event, if the government does not stimulate aggregate demand, and spontaneous inflation is present, the economy will experience less than full employment. This less than full employment position may be assumed terminal or temporary. In either case some output and employment would be foregone. Be it temporary or permanent, there would be attendant human suffering.

Within the cost-push framework the monetary mechanism is considered a passive force. But it cannot be ignored. Without increases in the money supply there could not be a permanent inflationary trend. Prices would rise for a time, then stop, for the

3. *Macroeconomic Theory* (New York: The Macmillan Company, 1961), pp. 445-46.

circulating velocity of money cannot rise without limit. In the cost-push terminology there is a policy choice, unemployment or inflation. By this it is meant that a higher average level of employment could be maintained through policies of inflationary finance than without, unless policy somehow ends the cost-push.

To the cost-push theorist, an initial cost rise results in the dilemma—unemployment or inflation. The government faced with such a situation has no choice but to maintain employment at the expense of mild, or perhaps not so mild, inflation.

In reply, the demand-pull theorist could argue that the government is not obligated to support high levels of employment at the expense of inflation because the public prefers, or should prefer, some unemployment to inflation, which is tantamount to the classical argument presented earlier that, in effect, the unemployment described by the cost-push theorist is not really unemployment—*i.e.*, full employment is that level of employment which is compatible with stable prices. In part, then, the whole argument hinges upon the efficacy of a policy solution; in part it is definitional in nature and probably rooted in differing value judgments. But in neither case is there presented a valid criticism of the cost-push hypothesis.

Thus the demand-pull theorist might better reply that cost inflation would not occur because businessmen, labor, and/or any other concerned group would not price in such a non-economic fashion. This raises the crucial issue of why aggregate supply should shift "spontaneously." Its analysis leads to a discussion of types of cost inflation.

One approach would be to couch the analysis in very general terms. This may be called the general cost-push inflation explanation. All prices (including the price of labor) rise at more or less the same rate. Why should this be so? Three explanations are likely: (1) It may be that the supply price increase of each product anticipates a future price (or cost) rise. (2) It may be that the supply price increase of each product represents an attempt to correct a previous inequity between factor prices and final prices. Examples are business pricing on a cost-plus basis (labor on a cost-of-living basis) and contractual obligations delaying a response. (3) It may be that those who generate inflationary pressures are not easily separated from those who do not. In such a case, policy makers would have to act *as if* the inflationary pressure were a general phenomenon affecting all sectors of the economy, even though this actually was not so.

For cases one and two, the historical question of how the phenomenon originated would not be deemed too important from a policy standpoint. Case number one, for example, might have originated as a result of anticipating demand-pull inflation or as a result of anticipating sector cost-push forces that led to general inflation. Case number two, again, might have started as a reaction, in this case a lagged reaction, to demand-pull or as a reaction to sector cost-push forces.

The important feature of either of these two types of general cost-push inflation is that even if the originating force, *e.g.*, excess aggregate monetary demand, were brought under control the general cost-push force would continue. Pricing conventions would have so solidified that the policy problem would have to be, how to deal with a general cost-push pressure even though, historically, the cause at first was not general cost-push.

The explanation of case number three is popularly attributed to the presence of administered prices. As DePodwin and Selden point out, the notion that administered prices are responsible for certain macro-economic problems is one of very long standing.[4] Originally the belief was that administered prices were rigid downward and hence contributed to the unemployment of the 1930's. The contemporary claim is that administered prices rise too quickly and, therefore, have contributed to recent inflationary experiences.[5]

Certainly, it may be concluded, the mere fact that administered prices exist does not explain why cost inflation of a general nature should occur. But the wide prevalence of administered prices does enable inflationary price-wage increases of the cost-push type. The

4. Horace J. DePodwin and Richard T. Selden, "Business Pricing Policies and Inflation," *Journal of Political Economy*, April, 1963, p. 116.

5. Both the earliest and the more recent formulations of administered price theory are associated closely with the name of Gardner C. Means. Two of his works are illustrative: *Industrial Prices and Their Relative Inflexibility*, Senate Document No. 13, January 17, 1935 (Washington: U.S. Government Printing Office, 1935) and *Pricing Power and the Public Interest: A Study Based on Steel* (New York: Harper and Bros., 1962). Two other discussions of note on the role of administered prices in the inflation process are: Otto Eckstein and Gary Fromm, *Steel and the Postwar Inflation*, study paper No. 2, prepared in connection with the study of employment, growth and price levels, U.S. Congress, Joint Economic Committee, 85th Cong., 1st Sess., 1959; and M. A. Adelman, "Steel Administered Prices and Inflation," *Quarterly Journal of Economics*, February 1961, pp. 16-40.

potential group of inflation initiators is large. The effects of their actions easily might spread throughout the economy and become quite general.

Given administered prices, the explanation of why some firms initiate price increases which give rise to general cost inflation pressures might follow either of two lines of approach. The explanation might hinge on the belief that increases by the initiating firms were unprofitable for them. Price increases which represent attempts to reach an unattainable profit goal are a plausible example. A more usual argument, however, is that the inflationary price increases would be profitable for the firms involved. But for this to be so, and assuming the increases are not to "correct" an existing or expected inequity between costs and prices, unexploited monopoly revenue must have existed. In Galbraithian terms there must have been unliquidated monopoly gain.[6]

Untapped monopoly revenue might be the result of any of several factors.[7] (1) It could be the consequence of imperfect knowledge on the part of business decision makers, as implied in the concept of mark-up inflation which Franklin D. Holzman,[8] Gardner Ackley,[9] and many others believe to be prevalent and potentially harmful to national price stabilization objectives. (2) It could be the consequence of a desire by businessmen to "save" some potential for profit through initially conservative pricing policies that would help assure a public record of continuous improvement in business performance over the years, or favorable performance during periods of economic adversity. In other words a "political" theory of managerial behavior parallel to the political theory of union wage demands Arthur Ross identified as motivating

6. J. K. Galbraith, "Market Structure and Stabilization Policy," *Review of Economics and Statistics*, May, 1957, pp. 124-34.

7. Specifically omitted from this sample listing is the possibility that those charged with the pricing of products, goods or services, are unaware of any output effect of price changes. One of the most frequent of lay observations must surely be the responsiveness of a change in quantity demanded to a change in price. Those who argue that businessmen and labor leaders ignore the employment or output effect of their actions must mean that said leaders do not consider this effect to be important. This conclusion can be reached only when the price change is moderate, when compared either with an absolute standard or with the actions of competitors, or when demand elasticity is low. In other situations output and employment effects would not be ignored.

8. "Income Determination in Open Inflation," *Review of Economics and Statistics*, May, 1950, pp. 150-58.

9. *Macroeconomic Theory*, pp. 452-59.

many trade union leaders.[10] (3) Or, finally, unliquidated monopoly revenue could be the consequence of conservative pricing out of fear of retaliatory anti-trust action or other public censure of "profiteering." This last is exemplified by those firms, which Braff and Miller believe are all too common, that are quite willing to grant liberal wage increases because of the excuse provided for excessive corporate price increases.[11]

A second kind of cost-push inflation theory (in addition to general cost-push) assumes that certain identifiable costs (prices) are crucial forces in the inflationary process. These "costs" may be some wages, as those which are union determined; specific raw material prices, as farm products; or product prices in key industries, as steel, automobiles, machine tools, or heavy goods as a group. Two arguments then are possible: (1) An initial rise in the key cost sector induces a "spiral" or "round" effect that influences the entire economy. (2) The key cost item is so large that any change in its price appreciably affects the general price-level.

In the case of the wage inflation thesis, if reference is to all wages and salaries, some two-thirds of National Income and 50-60 per cent of Gross National Product are encompassed. If all wages and salaries rise "spontaneously," to the extent that final prices reflect cost changes these wage and salary increases will have an inflationary impact. However, where the wage inflation thesis refers to wages alone, and not salaries, the hypothesis is less applicable if size and importance of the original increase is crucial. Moreover, if the argument is restricted to union wages alone, the thesis is limited sharply as only about one-third of those who work for wages are unionized.

If the wage inflation thesis presented suggests as culpable a small portion of the wage plus salary sector, *e.g.*, union determined wages, it must be that this sector induces others to follow. But this depends upon two supporting assumptions: (1) The group selected for blame must be in a better position than others to raise the price of its output and/or more powerfully motivated. The "political" theory of union wage demands is a reason why unions might behave this way. Excessive preoccupation with "produc-

10. *Trade Union Wage Policy* (Los Angeles: University of California Press, 1956).
11. Allan J. Braff and Roger F. Miller, "Wage-Price Policies Under Public Pressure," *Southern Economic Journal*, October, 1961, pp. 163-73.

tivity" wage increases even where market conditions do not warrant increases of this magnitude is another reason, supported by Paul Streeten,[12] why affected labor sectors might behave this way, union or non-union. (2) Although other groups cannot or will not initiate a rise in wages or prices, they respond with an increase when stimulated to do so by the key wage sector.

There are a number of similarities between the union wage inflation thesis and other forms of the "key cost" inflation theory. In each case it may be argued that the key sector alone measurably affects the general price level or that the key sector leads and other markets follow.[13] The relevant distinction for purposes of this paper is the policy issue: What is the key sector, and how effective are wage controls likely to be in the control of it, or of the inflation to which it leads?

Structuralist Inflation. A final inflation explanation, most thoroughly developed by Charles Schultze,[14] but supported by many others, stems from the contention that supply curves generally are not reversible and that patterns of demand continually fluctuate. In those areas where demand increases, relatively, prices rise as do output and employment. Where demand decreases prices remain approximately constant while output and employment fall. These associated decreases may be relative or absolute. Naturally the phenomenon to which Schultze refers long has been known to economists. It is, for example, inherent in discussion of the problems that price and wage inflexibility hold for economic management, factor mobility, and the like. What distinguishes the Schultze explanation from its fellows is that he has built an entire explanation of an inflationary period around the idea of dynamic markets and wage and price rigidities.

Thus, the secular upward drift to the price-level experienced

12. "Wages, Prices and Productivity," *Kyklos*, November, 1962, pp. 723-33.

13. The reasons why these sectors would engage in inflationary price increases are those mentioned earlier in connection with presentation of the general cost-push inflation argument.

14. While structuralist theories of inflation certainly owe their contemporary application to industrial economies largely to the efforts of Schultze, structuralist theories have been locally popular as an explanation for certain South American inflationary experiences for some time. See, for example, D. Seers, "A Theory of Inflation and Growth in Underdeveloped Countries," *Oxford Economic Papers*, 1962, pp. 173-95; as well as papers by Oliviera, Felix and Grunwald in *Latin American Issues: Essays and Comments*, Albert O. Hirschman, ed. (New York: Twentieth Century Fund, 1961).

from 1955 through 1957, and, presumably during certain other periods, under the Schultze argument is the result neither of over-all excess demand nor of spontaneous increases in prices and/or wages. Rather the explanation is to be seen from an examination of individual markets. Initially, in some sectors prices and wages rise because of a demand increase in those sectors. In certain other sectors prices and wages do not fall because of wage and price rigidities. Later, the initial upward drift of some prices and wages is communicated to most other areas of the economy. Higher prices become general because so many input costs have risen.

SIGNIFICANCE OF THE DISTINCTIONS AMONG THE HYPOTHESES

Available literature on theory of inflation cause leads to the assumption that different theories of price-level inflation cause would imply as most desirable at least partially different policy remedies. This, of course, is unfortunate because it is not known which theory is correct, or indeed that any one theory by itself is correct.

One means of obviating this dilemma would be to determine more precisely the cause or causes of inflation. Once this was done the search for an appropriate "cure" could begin in earnest. But there are a number of difficulties inherent in a search for inflation cause which at least for the present seem insuperable;[15] and even if the cause(s) of price-level inflation is (are) identified the search for a cure would remain.

For these reasons, this study will work in a second possible direction. It will move directly to examination of one possible inflation "cure"—national incomes policy. A primary reason will be to circumvent and move beyond existing discussions about inflation cause; but, although the approach avoids the question of cause, it has a bearing on that issue. The probable success of controls on wage bargaining both in those situations for which they were designed and in those for which they were not has definite relevance to the policy significance of inflation theories.[16]

15. Martin Bronfenbrenner and F. D. Holzman present an excellent discussion of some of these problems in their "Survey of Inflation Theory," *American Economic Review*, September, 1963, pp. 593-661, esp. pp. 630-39.

16. *Supra*, Chapter 12.

As indicated, evaluation of national incomes policy as a companion to appropriate monetary and fiscal policy for inflation control is the direct purpose of this book. The evaluation will be not only in light of the wage inflation thesis, which gave rise to the proposal for the wage control proposal, but also in light of the other four varieties of inflation theory discussed in this chapter: demand inflation, general cost-push inflation, "key" cost-push inflation, and Schultze type structuralist inflation. Answers to several questions are sought: (1) Can an incomes policy eliminate or reduce inflation of the wage-push type? (2) What will be the impact of such a policy on the rate of inflation if the inflationary experience is not entirely of the wage-push type? (3) What will be the probable costs and disadvantages to be expected from the use of incomes policy as an anti-inflationary device when inflation is wage-push in type, and when it is not?

Before the analysis moves to this aspect of the problem, however, it seems useful to digress briefly for the purpose of evaluating the impact of price-level inflation. The impact of price-level inflation is most relevant to the problem of evaluation of the incomes policy remedy because of the obvious necessity to understand the nature of the "evil" in order properly to appraise the worth of the "cure."

Chapter 4

THE PROBLEM OF INFLATION

THERE IS NO GENERAL AGREEMENT on the impact of price-level inflation. Most writers agree that the impact is bad.[1] Some, mavericks perhaps, do not accept even this initial premise. There is almost no agreement at all on the seriousness of the impact of inflation.

In addition to questions of fact, the diversity of observations regarding the relative desirability, or lack of it, of price-level inflation frequently can be traced to definitional discrepancies, implicit, or explicit, as well as disagreement as to appropriate economic ends.

Questions of fact undoubtedly account for much the greater portion of the controversy over impact. However a discussion of impact can be complicated by failure to designate the type of inflation referred to,[2] or by recognition of type and agreement on impact, but with disagreement as to whether the impact is good or bad.[3]

1. These men might accept inflation as a necessary concomitant of appropriate economic policies, but they regret the impact of inflation and accept it only because the policies which lead to inflation also lead to other, desirable, economic goals.

2. Discrepancies over the type of inflation which is referred to may center on type as classified by time series considered significant, price-level inflation, profit inflation, etc.; or by the character of the time series movement, broken versus unbroken trend inflation, anticipated versus unanticipated inflation, etc.

3. Chapter 2, "Employment and Inflation," touches on certain aspects of the problem of definition of goals.

Where the issue surrounds questions of fact it is the dual result of empirical and theoretical inadequacies. Available data do not indicate the true impact of price-level inflation. Indeed, available data are not always sufficiently accurate even to indicate if inflation is present, let alone its degree.[4] And, there is not one, but a variety of partially conflicting hypotheses as to the impact of price-level inflation. On the theoretical level there are two problems: (1) What was the initial inflation cause? (2) What is the nature of the response of the economy to the initial inflation stimulus?

From this it might seem that the previously discussed theories of inflation cause would shed a good deal of light on the nature of the impact of inflation. Actually they are not so helpful as might be supposed. With the exception of the Schultze explanation, these theories may be consistent with almost any conceivable impact of inflation. This is because existing theories of cause are structured to answer the question of what is the initial inflation cause, rather than what is the first variable to shift. But, for the purposes of analyzing the impact of inflation, the latter is likely to be a more meaningful issue.

It seems evident that the crucial issue for determining the impact of price-level inflation is the reaction of the economy to an initial cause. This aspect of the problem will be discussed first. It will be followed by a section dealing with the implications which cause would have for impact and another dealing with the impact of special types of price-level inflation as classified according to the character of the time series movement.

GENERAL IMPACT OF PRICE-LEVEL INFLATION

General objections to price-level inflation are of two types. One deals with impact on the producing sector, and the other with impact on relative income shares and on relative asset shares. As in-

4. This is a very real problem. It is estimated, for example, that since World War II as much as one-half of the increases in the Consumer Price Index may have been index error rather than actual price-level shifts. See the testimony of Dr. Raymond T. Bowman, Assistant Director for Statistical Standards, Bureau of the Budget, appearing on a panel discussion before the Joint Economic Committee, Subcommittee on Economic Statistics and citing some unpublished work of Allen Wallis of the University of Chicago; *Hearings, Part 2, Government Price Statistics*, 87th Cong., 1st Sess., May 1, 2, 3, 4, 5, 1961, pp. 766-67.

The economic consequences of wide-spread reliance upon such inaccurate

dicated earlier, both ignore the problem of international balance. It is assumed that the economy under study is relatively closed and/or capable of providing for international balance in some other way—by exchange rate adjustment, by trade restrictions, or by a flow of gold and currency reserves. Implications of inflation for the international sector, in the absence of alternative methods of adjustment, are discussed later in the chapter.

Impact of Inflation on the Level and Composition of Current Output. Leaving aside the problem of the international sector of the economy price-level inflation may result in higher, or lower, levels of current output than would have been achieved under price-level stability. Empirical data are not conclusive.

Inflation may stimulate current output, it is contended, by: (1) inducing anticipatory consumer buying, (2) bolstering investment incentive, and/or (3) stimulating factor supply.

An inflationary period, however mild, is said to result in some incentive for anticipatory consumer buying. Other things being equal, the amount of anticipatory buying that can be expected in a given period will be a function of the magnitude of increase in the inflation rate. However, the greater the anticipatory buying already undertaken, the greater the further acceleration of inflation required to increase the rate of advance consumer buying. Because of this, anticipatory buying is more likely to provide an initial impetus than to become a continuing source of stimulation for an economy.

The belief that inflation stimulates current output through provision of additional incentives to invest can be predicated upon any of several hypotheses: (1) Increased investment results from a lowered real rate of interest as potential lenders attempt a flight from money. (2) Anticipatory consumer buying induces new investment, the magnitude depending upon the degree of forward buying characteristic of the economy and the required capital/output ratio. (3) The expectation of a rise in investment costs encourages additional current investment. Naturally this is analogous to the case of advance consumer buying and is subject to a parallel criticism. It is unreasonable to expect unlimited investment in the

---

data are significant. The possibility now is raised that adjustments to inflation may occur when inflation is not even present, but merely indicated to be present by the data which are available.

absence of current need. (4) A wage lag during inflationary periods stimulates profits and therefore encourages new investment. But a wage lag, if it exists, does not assure an increase in profits; and a profit increase will not stimulate new investment if there is excess capacity.

The belief that inflation affects current output by stimulating factor supply also can be predicated upon a number of hypotheses: (1) Inflation reduces the real income of fixed income groups and encourages those previously idle to return to work.[5] But this ignores the variable income group and the question of whether their improved economic position may persuade them to work less or more. *A priori* reasoning indicates total employment might not change greatly; it might even decrease. (2) Members of the producing population, manufacturers or workers, are victims of money illusion. They will work harder during inflation than during periods of stable prices or deflation.[6] (3) Prices and wages are rigid downward but flexible upward. Given shifting patterns of demand, inflation facilitates resource allocation. This reasoning is akin to Slichter's when he concluded that mild inflation is probably a good thing. It stimulates the economy and the redistributive impact is not too harmful.[7] This argument also bears similarities to an argument as to inflation cause used by Charles L. Schultze and discussed in Chapter 3.[8]

The contention that inflation exerts a depressing influence on output denies the "stimulation" argument. Real demand declines

5. George L. Bach, *Inflation* (Providence: Brown University Press, 1958), p. 15.

6. Some who accept this hypothesis consider the result desirable because production is their paramount policy goal. Others contend that money illusion unfairly tricks workers into producing more than they otherwise would.

7. See, for example, U.S. Congress, Joint Economic Committee, *Hearings, Part I—The American Economy: Problems and Prospects,* pp. 2-53.

8. Actually this is the reverse of the Schultze position. The essence of Dr. Schultze's argument is that given prices and wages rigid downward, but flexible upward, some inflations are the result of efforts to shift resources in conformance with shifts in demand. A possible reversal of this argument would be that inflation results in more perfect resource allocation (instead of being the result of more perfect resource allocation). Although Schultze appears to view inflation as an effect rather than a cause, presumably he would not object to citing it as the independent variable. This would amount to saying that the Schultze analysis (i.e., some inflation is the result of pricing and wage-setting conventions) holds true only if the government inflates the money supply. If the government does not facilitate inflation in this way, less perfect resource allocation would result, as evidenced, in part, by unemployment.

to the extent that consumption expenditures are a planned dollar sum, to the extent that the progressive income tax reduces disposable income, to the extent that the real balance effect is operative, and to the extent that inflation redistributes income from those who emphasize consumption to those who emphasize saving. It is argued further that inflation works to reduce current output through: (1) introduction of greater uncertainty, and/or (2) creation of inefficiency.

The belief that inflation decreases current output through introduction of additional uncertainty can be illustrated simply. Assume a rate of inflation of 3 per cent per year anticipated by both a lender and a borrower, *i.e.,* the lender expects a rise in the general price level exactly equivalent to the increase that the investor expects. Assume a range of tolerance to the expectation. Assume further that the money rate of interest compensates for the predicted rate of inflation and no more. Given these assumptions plus a real rate of interest of 3 per cent for example, the lender ought not to loan at 6 per cent. With a declining marginal utility of money, the marginal disutility in case of loss would exceed the marginal utility in case of gain. The effective rate of interest would have to exceed 6 per cent for the lender to be interested.[9] Similarly, the borrower will want an anticipated real rate of return in excess of 3 per cent. He too must be compensated for uncertainty as to the expected magnitude of inflation.

The theory that inflation creates inefficiency assumes inflation distorts patterns of resource allocation. The arguments are several. Inflation makes the determination and maintenance of an equilibrium set of prices more difficult than it would be otherwise.[10] To the extent that inflation induces redistribution of income or asset holdings, it can be expected to affect consumption and invest-

9. A partially opposing point of view is to be found in Milton Friedman and L. J. Savage, "The Utility Analysis of Choices Involving Risk," *Journal of Political Economy*, August, 1948, pp. 279-304. This article is reprinted in American Economic Association, *Readings in Price Theory* (Homewood: Richard D. Irwin, 1952), pp. 57-96. It has been amended slightly by Harry Markowitz ("The Utility of Wealth," *Journal of Political Economy*, April, 1952, pp. 151-58), and tested favorably in Martin Weitzman ("Utility Analysis and Group Behavior: An Empirical Study," *Journal of Political Economy*, February, 1965, pp. 18-26). However, as Menehhem E. Yaari points out ("Convexity in the Theory of Choice Under Risk," *Quarterly Journal of Economics*, May, 1965, pp. 278-90) the whole controversy may center simply on variations in probability estimates.

10. This includes wages, since they are a form of prices.

ment patterns which would require adjustments. To the extent that
the rate of inflation differs from market to market, the adjustment
process will be even more difficult. Inflation encourages speculation, another complicating factor. Inflation also is characterized by
leads and lags, associated with too little investment attention devoted to some markets and too much to others.

*Impact of Inflation on the Level and Composition of Secular
Output.* Some who accept the hypothesis that inflation stimulates
current output assert that this stimulation is undesirable because
of implications for secular output. There are two major com-
plaints: (1) Although current output may be stimulated, the rise
is temporary and eventually leads to interruption in growth. (2)
The composition of current output, after inflation, especially
hampers growth.

Professor Fellner[11] presents the first point of view very well.
According to Fellner, the primary impact of inflation is a temporary
stimulus to current output which cannot be maintained. As the
economy returns to "normal," an interruption in growth, which
leads to deflation becomes inevitable. Fellner has in mind anticipatory buying that will not be maintained, the need for revision
of the structure of production which existing mobility of resources
cannot provide within an acceptable time period (as temporary
investment spurts come to an end), and the like.

To oppose the Fellner view, it is necessary to argue either that
the increase in current output would continue indefinitely or that
inflation, which leads to deflation, is helpful to economic development. One might reason *a la* Slichter that inflation improves resource allocation and therefore stimulates progress and development, or one might use the "pump priming" framework. Alternatively, as Schumpeter argues:[12] ". . . cycles are essential elements of
the mechanism of economic development and cannot be eliminated
without crippling the latter."

David McCord Wright points out,[13] and Schumpeter appears
to agree, that at least for post 1918 cycles,[14] this "purgative" theory

11. William Fellner, *Trends and Cycles in Economic Activity.*

12. J. A. Schumpeter, *The Theory of Economic Development* (Cambridge:
Harvard University Press, 1949), p. 253.

13. "Moulton's the New Philosophy of Public Debt," *American Economic
Review*, September, 1943, p. 587.

14. J. A. Schumpeter, *Business Cycles* (New York: McGraw-Hill, 1939), pp.
153-55.

of the business cycle is a special case only because the downswing is likely to go beyond the point of any usefulness and, by its adverse effects, negate the purgative value of a recession.

The second point of view, that the composition of current output after inflation may inhibit growth, assumes that inflation creates inefficiency, and/or causes resources to be shifted from capital formation. Possible explanations of this hypothesis include an increase in uncertainty because of inflation and a reduction in the incentive to lend because of a reduced real rate of interest.

Disturbance of consumption patterns associated with a delayed real balance effect presents still another force on the side of interruption of secular output. That is, at first when prices are rising total spending may rise as individuals and businesses engage in anticipatory buying as a hedge against still more inflation in the future. Eventually, however, the expectational purchases decline in intensity as stocks of goods held by the public rise to the point where further anticipatory buying would be uneconomical (the cost of holding stocks of goods becomes excessive). Savings then rise (spending falls) as a consequence of a general effort to re-build cash balances whose purchasing power earlier had been impaired by inflation and where size was impaired by profligate spending.

Impact of Inflation on Relative Shares. A priori reasoning can lead to a variety of conclusions about the net impact of inflation on the producing sector, depending upon the nature of the initial assumptions employed. But many writers who acknowledge this uncertainty, vehemently oppose inflation. They consider the redistributional impact of inflation on relative incomes and asset holdings the more important consequence of an inflationary movement. Thus the question is posed: What is the impact of inflation on relative income and asset shares and does the uncertainty that surrounds the impact of inflation on production necessarily surround the impact of inflation on relative shares?

It might seem that the redistributional impact of inflation is clearly definable. Other things remaining equal, inflation (1) redistributes real purchasing power from those whose money incomes rise less rapidly to those whose money incomes rise more rapidly than the rate of inflation and (2) from those whose assets (valued in money terms) rise less rapidly than the rate of inflation to those whose assets rise more rapidly.

But, if an effort is made to determine whose incomes (or assets) are relatively fixed in money value, or if no assumptions are made as to inflation cause, consideration of the impact of inflation on relative shares is fully as inconclusive as consideration of the impact on the producing sector. It is uncertain, for example, whether inflation is redistributional from rich to poor, from poor to rich, from old to young, or from young to old.

To illustrate, frequently mentioned as a group that loses, relatively, during an inflationary period are persons on pension. But pension benefits may be subject to change over time. They may be scaled upward out of charity or because the rate of return on asset value exceeded expectations. In fact inflation often induces an enlarged return.

IMPACT OF INFLATION UPON THE INTERNATIONAL SECTOR

Obviously the impact of domestic inflation upon a country's international account depends upon many factors—most notably upon how open is the economy in question[15] and what reliance typically can be placed upon methods other than regulation of aggregate monetary demand to achieve and maintain balance in the country's international sector. Because of these factors it is very difficult to generalize as among nations when considering the impact of inflation upon the international sector. For some countries the impact may be large, for others quite small. Nonetheless, a case may be made for saying there is a tendency to over-dramatize the impact of domestic inflation upon a country's balance of payments position. Recent experiences of the United States seem illustrative of the point.

Since World War II the rate of inflation in the United States has been lower than that of any other advanced, industrialized nation. But the general view still seems to be that price level increases in the U. S. have serious, as opposed to moderate, balance of payments implications. Perhaps this is because domestic price-level adjustment represents a possible, albeit very unsatisfactory, method

15. Of course, even relatively open economies may not be much affected by internal inflation so far as their international accounts are concerned. Everything really depends not only upon total quantities of international trade (as a percentage of Gross National Product) but also upon the relative elasticity of demand for the country's output together with the country's marginal propensity to import, as a function of price and income change.

for restoration of "equilibrium" in the international sector. Or perhaps it is because domestic inflation can add to an already difficult balance of payments problem. In any event, for the United States at least, the case seems overdrawn.

According to one study, a rate of inflation three per cent in excess of the average of price-level increases experienced by the European and Asian nations with whom the U.S. does most of its trading[16] would add no more than a billion dollars to the balance of payments deficit.[17] Since other countries also are experiencing inflation a three per cent excess inflation would require an actual cumulation much above that. And a billion dollars worth of change in the U. S. international accounts would be relatively insignificant, were it not for mounting problems already experienced as a direct inheritance of a thirty-year policy of no change in the exchange value of the dollar and full convertibility with gold.

IMPLICATIONS OF INFLATION CAUSE
FOR IMPACT

The relationship between inflation cause and impact is a close one. This section aims at a sketch of the implications for impact of existing theories of cause. Apart from the obvious desire to clarify the relationship between cause and impact, the discussion is requisite to later judgments about the value of governmentally proscribed limits to private bargaining over wages in particular inflation situations.

As will be seen, the influence of cause on impact is obscure. This is because sector by sector reaction to an inflation stimulus may lead, lag behind or be approximately simultaneous with the actual inflation cause. It was explained earlier that the data are not conclusive.[18] There are times when producer-goods prices appear to have shifted first with consumer-goods prices and wages shifting later. But there is no evidence to indicate that this re-

16. This analysis is based upon the assumption that Canada, much of South America and certain other countries are tied so closely to the United States through trade relations that they must follow the U. S. economy very closely. The three per cent figure assumes that these nations will inflate and deflate in a manner approximately parallel to the United States.

17. Charles T. Haworth, "Estimates of the Effects of Devaluation on U.S. Balance of Payments" (Unpublished Ph.D. dissertation, Department of Economics, University of Oregon, 1968).

18. *Supra*, p. 30.

lationship always holds true. The validity of the generalization is open to considerable question.[19]

As with the earlier discussion, two aspects of impact need to be considered: impact of inflation cause on the producing sector, impact on relative income and relative asset shares. No differential impact on the international sector is considered relevant. The five general theories of cause treated are those outlined in Chapter 3: demand-pull inflation; three types of cost-push inflation, general cost-push, wage-push, "key" cost-push; and Schultze-type structural inflation.

Impact of Demand-Pull Inflation. The concept of demand-pull inflation might be associated with final product prices moving upward first, intermediate product prices and certain labor costs rising next, and raw material prices following last. In each individual market situation excess demand would appear, temporary shortages would develop, and prices would respond by moving upward.

This demand-pull theory implies a wage lag. It implies expanded profits also. These changes would be associated with a greater incentive to invest than otherwise would occur. Further, this theory implies some industries, *e.g.,* consumers' goods industries, fare better than others, e.g., producers' goods industries. As a final implication, this demand-pull theory would be associated with changes in income distribution, relative increases in the return to capital, and relative decreases to labor.

As an alternative to the above, demand-pull inflation might be characterized by wages and prices moving upward more or less simultaneously in all markets. That is, there would be no particular bias which would foster a wage lag for example. The argument here could be that shifts in market demand generally are anticipated adequately and that market prices shift more or less simultaneously with changes in aggregate monetary demand.

As a final possibility, demand-pull inflation could be associated with prices in factor markets leading those in final product markets. Two explanations for this are possible. It may be that factor price changes anticipate changes in aggregate monetary demand and move to meet these changes more quickly than do final product prices. As another possibility, some markets may follow a rigid cost

19. Reuben A. Kessel and Armen A. Alchian, "The Inflation-Induced Lag of Wages," *American Economic Review,* March, 1960, pp. 43-66.

plus set mark-up pricing policy, while others, labor for example, do not. Then demand-pull again would be characterized by an initial price rise elsewhere than in the final product market.

The impact of anticipated demand-pull, of course, would be the reverse of that suggested as a first possibility. Wages would lead, not lag. Profits would be lower than otherwise and incentive to invest, therefore, would be reduced. Redistributional changes associated with the demand inflation also would be reversed. Labor would be expected to gain, relatively, while capital owners would be expected to lose.

Unfortunately, when it comes to assessing the empirical validity of a wage or price lead, an especially confusing aspect is that demand-pull induced lags may be so great that they could be confused with leads and, of course, the converse of this also is true. Further, the discussion thus far has assumed that, whatever the impact of demand inflation, it follows one of the three patterns suggested above. If, instead, some markets are characterized by profit leads, others by lags, etc., then the impact would depend upon the ratio of leads to lags.

Impact of Cost-Push Inflation. Possibilities surrounding the impact of cost-push inflation parallel those explored in connection with the demand-pull case and are equally diverse. If the inflation is general cost-push in type, wages and producers' goods prices may move up before final product prices. Alternatively, manufacturers of final products may forecast a cost-push force and change their prices simultaneously or in anticipation of it.

Insofar as theory of impact is concerned, the contribution of varieties of cost inflation theory other than general cost-push is largely one of focusing attention on some particular variable(s). "Key" cost inflation focuses attention on the relationship of the "key" cost area to the balance of the economy. Wage-push inflation emphasizes wage-price relationships. In each case, however, reaction by the economy may lead, lag behind, or shift simultaneously with the initiating cost change. Or, an even more likely case, the response of the economy may be a mixture of all three possibilities.

Impact of Schultze-Type Structural Inflation. The Schultze inflation explanation implies bottlenecks with prices and wages rising in these sectors more than elsewhere. Of course the composition of the bottleneck group is shifting all the time but this is more an empirical than a theoretical problem. The Schultze inflation explanation is much less amenable to alternative interpretation as to its impact than either the demand-pull explanation or any of the cost-push theories. This is because the issue of anticipated change is less relevant. Those markets which experience increasing demand are characterized by increasing prices. Whether these prices move in anticipation of a change in market demand or as a lagged reaction to change in market demand does not adjust the final conclusion—the prices rise. For those markets which are characterized by price stability in the face of declining demand, the question of anticipations is irrelevant for analysis of price-level movements—prices do not move.

To some extent, however, Schultze inflation becomes general when price rises in bottleneck sectors are communicated to other markets through the medium of cost increases. To the degree that this is the case, these cost increases may lead, lag behind, or be simultaneous with the associated price changes in other markets. Each case has the earlier discussed consequences for impact.

IMPACT OF SPECIFIC TYPES OF INFLATION

Many writers consider certain types of inflation particularly objectionable. These qualified objections to inflation merit discussion both as an aid to understanding the nature of the impact of inflation and the range of disagreement concerning it.

Anticipated and Unanticipated Inflation. One "qualified" objection to inflation centers on the degree to which it is anticipated. If an inflationary experience occurs which is repetitive this may add to expectations for further inflation. If so, individuals could be expected to reappraise their producing and consuming habits, and the impact of future inflation could be altered considerably.

Abba Lerner exemplifies the economist who is concerned with whether or not the inflation is anticipated. As Lerner explains it, the harmful effects of inflation result not from the rise in prices *per se*, ". . . but [from] the failure to anticipate and offset them."[20] Thus, says Lerner, concern should not be with expected inflation. For the economic man this represents more of a harassment than a social evil.

20. Abba Lerner, *et al.*, "The Inflationary Process," a symposium, *Review of Economics and Statistics*, August, 1949, p. 194.

Anticipated inflation requires that an additional factor, expected rate of inflation, be incorporated into the analysis, and compensation for this variable takes some effort. However, anticipated inflation can be compensated for and hence it does not, says Lerner, result in the more serious charges usually attributed to inflation in general.[21]

Exception to the Lerner position has come from several sources,[22] but fundamentally the complaint is that anticipation of inflation causes a revised attitude toward the holding of cash balances, as the store of value function is less adequately served. The result is a flight from money to bonds and, perhaps, to consumption. Market rates of interest do not rise by a margin equal to the rate of inflation expected, and saving habits may be changed also.

But Phelps points out that the true outcome depends upon specific assumptions regarding the monetary and fiscal policy mix.[23] And, in any event, to some extent early cash balance erosion may be offset by the operation of a real balance effect later. Once the real value of cash balances has fallen substantially because of rising prices, cash balances will need to be rebuilt. Interest rates, and perhaps savings, will rise, rather than fall.

But all this seems to beg the main point. Lerner did not contend that anticipated inflation would be without its effects. His real claim was that free markets may adjust to anticipated inflation. This makes the impact of anticipated inflation different, and much less objectionable, than otherwise would be the case.

Mild Inflation and Rapid Inflation. A second "qualified" objection to inflation centers on whether the inflation is mild or rapid in intensity. Many more writers object to rapid inflation than object to mild inflation. The belief seems to be that the stimu-

---

21. Although he does not specifically say so, when Lerner formulated this analysis, he apparently was thinking of mild trend inflation.

22. See, Milton Friedman, "Discussion of the Inflationary Gap," *Essays in Positive Economics* (Chicago: University of Chicago Press, 1953), pp. 253-62; Martin J. Bailey, "The Welfare Cost of Inflationary Finance," *Journal of Political Economy*, June, 1963, pp. 93-110; Robert M. Mundell, "Inflation and Real Interest," *Journal of Political Economy*, June, 1963, pp. 280-83; Edmund S. Phelps, "Anticipated Inflation and Economic Welfare," *Journal of Political Economy*, February, 1965, pp. 1-17; and Alvin L. Marty, "Growth and the Welfare Cost of Inflationary Finance," *Journal of Political Economy*, February, 1967, pp. 71-76.

23. *Ibid.*

lating benefits of inflation are more likely to be offset by the disruptive effects if the inflation is rapid.

Of those who object to mild inflation, some do so because they believe mild inflation leads to anticipation of inflation, and anticipation of inflation leads people to take compensating action which leads to an intensification of inflation. These writers contend it is immaterial whether mild inflation is beneficial. Mild inflation cannot long stay mild. It leads to more rapid inflation and eventually, perhaps, to hyper-inflation.[24]

But *a priori* reasoning does not provide adequate grounds for concluding that mild inflation must inevitably transmute to more rapid inflation. This conclusion will hold even if it is assumed that inflation is anticipated. Individuals may be victims of money illusion, for example. On the other hand, neither does *a priori* reasoning provide adequate grounds for concluding that mild inflation usually will remain mild.

Broken and Unbroken Inflation. A third category of objections to inflation surrounds the issue of broken versus unbroken inflation, that is inflation of the "stair-step" variety which occurs as a result of any of several policy activities. It can result from anti-depression policies unmatched by anti-inflationary policies of equal intensity, an attempt to maintain over-full employment in the Ohlin sense of available jobs in excess of the number of applicants willing and able to work, or an effort always to maintain a minimum of full employment resulting in accidental instances of over-full employment.

It is possible to argue that broken trend inflation is not inflation in the same sense as unbroken trend inflation. One reason is that broken trend inflation could occur as a result of efforts to eliminate Keynesian unemployment by monetary means. Inflation then would be the price of creating the improved employment situation, and under these circumstances an absence of any balance of payments consequences would be expected. That is, balance of payments consequences usually would occur only under the condition of a world depression, where domestic price declines would be necessary simply for a country to maintain its relative position in world trade. Even then devaluation would be an alternative.

In general, examination of the broken trend inflation and

24. See, for example, Neil Jacoby, *Can Prosperity Be Sustained?* (New York: Henry Holt, 1956), p. 27.

unbroken trend inflation cases simply reinforces the main conclusion that inflation may arise from a variety of causes and that some types of inflation may be more difficult to eliminate than others. With the exception of the Keynesian unemployment case, there seems no evidence to indicate that the impact of broken trend inflation on patterns and levels of output or income is any different from that of unbroken trend inflation.

Open Inflation and Repressed Inflation. It is occasionally argued that although open inflation may be harmful in its effects, repressed inflation is not so objectionable. But whenever direct controls are used as a prime anti-inflationary device and are not supported adequately by the use of general monetary and fiscal controls, there still is the excess demand that often is characteristic of inflation. The difference is that the excess demand is evidenced by something other than the upward movement of a price, wage or profit index.

Use of direct controls to deal with a general excess of monetary purchasing power results in numerous problems. Sometimes these are the same as those usually associated with open inflation, *e.g.*, the altered pattern of resource allocation characteristic of open inflation; sometimes they are different; but even when different they can be expected to be no less acute. One problem that repressed inflation is not associated with so greatly is balance of payments.

INFLATION IN THE AMERICAN ECONOMY

Price inflation data, even that currently being compiled, are most inaccurate. But, the data do indicate the United States has been faced with the problem of inflation since its inception. The experience, of course, is not unique. In recent years, moreover, measured inflation in the United States has been comparatively mild as contrasted with instances in the past and with contemporary experiences of other nations.

There has been in the history of the U. S. one notable instance of hyper-inflation, in the South during the Civil War, as well as inflationary experiences of milder intensity. Northern experience during the Civil War and U. S. experience immediately after World War I might be characterized as instances of "rapid" inflation, while examples of "mild" inflation are common. Of course comparisons of this sort are difficult and results only approximate, as available evidence is limited and often conflicting. Only the most casual data concerning this nation's early years are available. Most of that is yearly only. In addition, in the past regional variations in economic activity have been even more acute than at present. Thus what is said of the nation may not be at all true of certain areas, and the converse is also true.

Perhaps the best example of mild trend inflation is the post World War II era. Since 1947 measured consumer prices have risen about 42 per cent, or an average of a little under 2.0 per cent per annum. Only two periods since 1947 clearly fall outside the range most would term mild inflation and both of these, 1947-48 with a 6.4 per cent increase in the Consumer Price Index and 1950-51 with an 8.0 per cent increase, were brief. A few also might consider the 1956-57 period one of rapid inflation, as measured consumer prices rose a little under 3.5 per cent during this period. But all in all the U.S. experience for the post World War II period compares favorably with the situation in virtually any foreign nation and certainly with all of the advanced industrialized countries of the world. In addition the U.S. experience for this period falls well within the range of what most refer to as mild inflation.

The best statistical information bearing on the impact of inflation in the United States is that collected in the past two or three decades. For this reason analysis of the impact of inflation must be an analysis of the impact of mild inflation. Further, this mild inflation may have been any of several types, as classified by cause. Existing knowledge of inflation is not adequate to determine past causes.

Examination of the U.S. data during the past few decades suggests that: (1) output and inflation are positively correlated both cyclically and secularly; and (2) although the distributive impact is exceptionally difficult to appraise, it seems not to have been extensive. Analysis of changes in relative factor shares from 1939-52, for example, indicates that during this period labor gained a little (plus 6 per cent), business firms lost just slightly (minus 4 per cent) as did dividend income groups (minus 2 per cent), while transfer payments showed some slight improvement (plus 1 per cent).[25] Thus, on the basis of one possible schema of disaggregation, measurable net changes in relative factor shares in the United

25. G. L. Bach and Albert Ando, "The Redistributional Effects of Inflation," *Review of Economics and Statistics*, February, 1957, p. 3.

States were not large during an extended period of mild trend inflation. However, neither this conclusion nor the statement about the positive correlation between output and inflation is at all certain. The data are not that conclusive.

The relationship between recent inflationary experiences and changes in relative factor shares is uncertain. Therefore, the relevance of relative share data to the present issue is suspect. The veracity of available empirical observations also is undetermined. It is difficult to disentangle the effects of inflation from the effects of other forces. And techniques of disaggregation may hide the "true" impact of changes which inflations induce. The impact of inflations is almost certain to cut across lines of income or wealth grouping of businesses and individuals. This makes quantification of the results difficult.

It is not surprising that those statistical studies made have yielded highly inconclusive results as to the "true" impact of inflation.[26] Simply stated, the import of this is that the hypotheses discussed earlier in the chapter concerning possible effects of inflation are with few exceptions reasonable possibilities. By way of partial qualification, however, the data do indicate that mild inflation can be maintained for considerable periods of time without necessarily leading to rapid inflation, much less to hyper-inflation.[27]

26. In addition to Bach and Ando see, for example, Harold Wolozin, "Inflation and the Price Mechanism," *Journal of Political Economy*, October, 1959, pp. 463-75; Reuben A. Kessel, "Inflation Caused Wealth Redistribution: A Test of a Hypothesis," *American Economic Review*, March, 1956, pp. 128-42; G. D. N. Wordswick, "Prices, Productivity, and Incomes," *Oxford Economic Papers*, June, 1958, pp. 246-64; Boris P. Pesek, "Distribution Effects of Inflation and Taxation," *American Economic Review*, March, 1960, pp. 147-53; as well as a considerable quantity of material put out by the U.S. Congress, Joint Economic Committee in 1958 and 1959 including: *Staff Report on Employment, Growth, and Price Levels*, December 24, 1959, esp. Chapter V.; Seymour E. Harris, *The Incidence of Inflation: Or Who Gets Hurt?* (Study Paper No. 7), November 26, 1959; H. S. Houtaker, *Protection Against Inflation* (Study Paper No. 8), November 24, 1959; and *The Relationship of Prices to Economic Stability and Growth* (Compendium of papers), March 31, 1958, especially the papers by Bloom, Bodenhorn, Christ, Eckstein, and Lewis.

27. An explanation for this phenomenon in the form of a study of consumer attitudes toward inflation may be found in Eva Muller, "Consumer Reactions to Inflation," *Quarterly Journal of Economics*, May 1959, pp. 246-62. Reuben A. Kessel and Armen A. Alchian also point out that on the purely theoretical level expectations of inflation call for consumer reactions but these adjustments once made will not accelerate unless the rate of inflation does also: "Effects of Inflation," *Journal of Political Economy*, December, 1962, pp. 521-37.

PART II

Wage Inflation Situations

Chapter 5

THE PROPOSAL TO BE EXAMINED

THIS CHAPTER begins what might be termed the major effort. It introduces Part II which is devoted to the central question posed: Can a national incomes policy in conjunction with appropriate monetary and fiscal arrangements effectively combat wage inflation?

As earlier suggested, the requirements of a suitable program are several: (1) It must not hinder, and if possible should reinforce, price-stabilizing monetary and fiscal policy. (2) It must not cause misallocation of resources and/or distortion of income distribution to a greater extent than that combination of unemployment and/or inflation which is believed to be alternative. (3) It must not so alter incentives and attitudes as drastically to affect the nature of the economic system.

These are difficult and rather specialized criteria. As a consequence, although the worlds both of theory and of practice abound with wage control programs, many or most of which have at least some anti-inflation effect, if not intent, the relevance of these ideas and programs to the major question often is slight. The difficulty is that so few of the programs now in practice or under discussion are designed for the control of wage inflation. Those that do have this objective often fail to provide for its accomplishment within the context of modern economic goals and existing free enterprise institutions including price stabilizing monetary and fiscal policy, and relative wage flexibility in response to shifting market conditions.

CHARACTER OF THE WAGE INFLATION FORCE

The obvious purpose of national incomes policy as an anti wage inflation device is to limit any inflation pressure without creating evils as great as or greater than those which would exist in the absence of the developed system of controls. The importance of this objective requires inquiry into the reasons underlying advocacy of national incomes policy as a companion to monetary and fiscal policy for inflation control.

The idea of governmentally established limits to private bargaining over wages as a means by which to combat wage-price inflation hinges upon certain basic assumptions, beliefs, ideas. To understand such an inflation "cure" it is necessary to understand the general point of view which underlies it.

From the standpoint of scope of the problem, there were outlined in Part I two broad types of wage-push possibilities which might occur separately or, perhaps, in concert, and for which incomes policy might be a remedy. (1) Wage inflation pressures might be confined to a particular market sector. Or, (2) wage inflation pressures might be general, affecting most or nearly all markets.

Wage inflation theories that place the blame for inflation initiation on the behavior of only a sector of the labor market are almost infinitely varied in the causes cited and sectors named. For instance the offending sector might be distinguished only by the craft or skill characteristics of the labor involved, as for example all the skilled or the unskilled workers. Or the offending sector might be composed of workers in a particular industry, as for example steel or auto workers. Or again, the offending sector might represent a control center, as workers with a union affiliation.

Although possible variations are not quite so numerous, inflation theories that place the blame on general instead of specific wage inflation pressures also can be based on any of several contentions. Perhaps, for example, all or nearly all labor markets share in the blame for initiating an inflationary round. Alternatively, perhaps the inflation cause is general only in the sense that inflation pressures in a few markets have become common because of imitative effects, the so-called spiral or round of inflation in other words. As still another alternative, it may be that responsibility for inflation shifts continually and unpredictably among sectors of the labor market.

The number of labor markets responsible for initiating wage inflation pressures is relevant to the inflation control problem for it bears upon the scope of the controls that are needed. General wage inflation implies need for controls on all wages. Sector wage inflation suggests a more limited control program. Of course, sector wage inflation could be prevented by partial controls only if intervention in the "offending" markets successfully forestalled general wage increases. This is a difficult requirement and may be especially so in some instances, as where composition of the initiating sector is a shifting one. Nonetheless, sector controls could be of considerable value in proper situations.

Sector controls could permit a degree of regulation by comparison, not possible where more general controls are used. Sector controls could reduce the scope and therefore the magnitude of the wages administration task. And sector controls could be less perfect than general controls need be, as adverse effects of the control program would be felt by only a portion of the economy, primarily the regulated portion.

In addition to variations in the number of labor markets believed responsible for initiating wage inflation pressures, wage inflation theories also differ in causes emphasized.

For example, some theories emphasize high wage demands, facilitated by the "excessive" bargaining power of labor, as a chief wage inflation cause. Others emphasize worker preoccupation with money illusion, which takes the form of resistance to money wage decreases. Still others emphasize over-ambitious union leaders who use unduly aggressive bargaining as a means of justifying their existence to rank-and-file membership.

The cause underlying an inflationary wage bargain also is relevant to the control program, for it affects the structure of the controls needed. For example, the overambitious union leader theory may imply a recommendation that union leaders ought not to be permitted an important role in any wage setting program. The "excessive" bargaining idea seems to suggest the legal curtailment of trade unions. And worker preoccupation with money illusion logically may call for an improved educational program, perhaps combined with retraining and other devices to increase worker mobility and thereby ease the need for downward wage flexibility to promote such adjustments.

Not every wage inflation theory suggests the same sort of

remedy as most relevant. Equally, no single palliative can remedy all forms of wage inflation. Nonetheless, some wage inflation remedies clearly are more general than others, and fundamental principles of wage inflation control can be developed which are widely applicable.

With regard to the scope of the controls, any set of criteria that is satisfactory to the determination of all wages and relies upon the same sort of wage determination criteria as the free market, would be applicable to some or all wage sectors of the economy.

Concerning inflation cause any set of criteria that independently indicates correct wage levels and patterns, would be applicable to a variety of wage inflation situations. Partly this is so because control implementation procedures need not rely heavily upon those who are believed to be important contributors to the inflation process. More importantly it is because only two causes are fundamental to most wage inflation theories: excessive bargaining power of labor and downward wage rigidities. Theories of inflation cause commonly vary only in the ratio of importance assigned to these two causes or in the explanation of the origin of the causes. Control possibilities that deal with these two problems thus would enjoy wide applicability.

CONTROL POSSIBILITIES

Logically, the first step toward selection of a control program appropriate for relief of wage inflation pressures might seem to be a study of methods employed by countries using some form of direct controls on wages. Certainly the list of countries that employ extensive controls on wages is long. It embraces all of the Communist and Communist Satellite nations; a majority of the so-called underdeveloped nations, including all of Central America and a majority of South America, Africa, the Middle East, and Non-Communist Asia; a few of the British Commonwealth nations, notably India and Australia; plus a great deal of Western Europe, including most of the Benelux and all of the Scandinavian countries as well as Austria, Spain and Portugal. In addition controls are found in numerous smaller nations such as Iceland, as well as in areas which might be classified as borderline in the sense that the control programs used are somewhat less elaborate—the United Kingdom, Italy, and France, for instance.

The difficulty with studying other countries is that the purpose of their controls usually is not that of regulating wage inflation within the context of price-stabilizing monetary and fiscal policy. There is a wide choice of possible types of wage control available to the policy maker and the above cited list of countries is representative of this breadth of choice. Not only do control techniques of the above listed countries vary in legislated structure, but in administrative techniques, and intensity of their application as well. Some controls are of the type that place a ceiling on wages only; others place a floor under wages. Some of the controls are partial in nature, others more general. Some of the wage control programs are relatively flexible in operation; others are not. And some of the control policies concentrate solely on the regulation of relative wage rates, while others involve regulation of relative wages only to the extent needed for control of the aggregate wage bill.

The several techniques available for wages control are capable of yielding markedly different results. Hence, the alternate programs are not perfect substitutes for each other. Not only do they fail to fill the requirements of a suitable program for wage inflation control equally well, but some hardly can be said to accomplish the objective at all. Two examples should serve to heighten this point.

(1) Wage floors (minimum wage) and the less common wage ceilings probably are best designed to adjust the pattern of relative wage rates. They are wholly unsuited to wage inflation control.

(2) World War II type wage controls, which allow for little or no flexibility in relative wage rates and/or in the general level of wages, have as their primary objective maintenance of the status quo. They will work best to contain short period inflationary pressures that do not evidence a strong bias towards particular labor markets. They are unsuited to long term application in the context of a dynamic economy where absolute and relative income shares of the various factors of production ought to be shifting continually.

For control of trend inflation with a wage-push cause, the incomes policy program most likely to be needed would work to control the aggregate wage bill within the bounds of price-stabilizing monetary and fiscal policy. But it should still permit changes in wage patterns in response to the ebb and flow of the demand for labor relative to its supply in the different sectors of the economy. This is not to say, of course, that wage controls of this kind will be positively helpful. But herein lies the most logical possibility.

CRITERIA FOR IMPLEMENTATION

Once the broad outline of the control program has been established, it is necessary to develop suitable criteria for its implementation. This is a knotty and important issue. It is upon the matter of criteria for implementation that the success or failure of national incomes policy as an anti wage inflation device is quite likely ultimately to depend.

Few American economists have directed their attention towards theoretical development of a control program tailored to the specialized conditions just outlined. Practically without exception, those who have attempted this task either have considered it peripheral to their main purpose of developing available cost inflation theory, or else have confined themselves to the limited objective of suggesting possibilities rather than presenting a detailed control proposal.

In the United States, national incomes policy takes the form of informal rules contained in the President's "Guideposts to Non-Inflationary Wage Bargaining."[1] Of the national incomes policy rules that might be studied these are perhaps the best for present purposes. The guideposts are interesting because through them the attention of American economists and others has been directed to the national incomes policy idea. They are interesting also because of the discussion and analysis that have been generated over the specific control principle which is fundamental to their operation.[2] The President's guideposts thus are an expression of the proposal to be examined by this work. They provide the point of departure for the analysis which follows. The guideposts which are in two parts can be summarized fairly briefly.

The first part is the general guidepost that the rate of increase in wage rates, including fringe benefits, should equal the rate

1. First proposed by President Kennedy in January of 1962, the "guideposts" were reprinted in the *Economic Report of the President* for that year, and have appeared in each *Economic Report* since that time.
2. See, for example, Charles E. Rockwood, "What's Wrong with the Wage Guideposts," *Business Horizons*, Spring, 1966, pp. 25-34; Alan Greenspan, "Those Battered Guideposts," *Challenge Magazine*, September, 1966, pp. 38-41, 50-51;

of increase in real output per man-hour over the nation. The general guidepost is supposed to indicate the average of wage settlements. Deviations are acceptable in particular industries, indeed may be essential, but the deviations should balance out to the general guidepost. Moreover, it is contended, the typical wage settlement will not deviate from the general guidepost, which will apply in the majority of situations. It seems to be taken as a working hypothesis that the general guidepost in practice will amount to a little over three per cent per year.

The second part is the modifications designed to indicate the situations in which a wage settlement ought to deviate from the guidepost norm. The modifications call for wage increases faster than the norm in an industry characterized by (a) a labor shortage and/or (b) wage rates well below those paid elsewhere to labor of similar ability. Symmetrically, increases in wage rates would be below the norm indicated by the general guidepost if the industry is characterized by (a) a labor surplus and/or (b) wages well above those paid elsewhere to labor of similar ability.

The macro rule of wages adjusted in accordance with general shifts in output per worker (sometimes called productivity change) is attractive for two reasons. First is the degree to which it suggests conformance with the objective of wage policy compatible with price stabilizing monetary and fiscal policy. Second is the promise held forth of no unwarranted interference with existing patterns of income distribution to the various factors of production, land, labor and capital.

The idea that wage trends should follow productivity gains is not new, although it is controversial. Its history is rooted in the now lengthy debate among economists over the actual and the appropriate trend in labor's relative income share.

Implications of the relative shares debate for the choice of wage level objectives are important and require examination. Also important is examination of the consequences, for stabilization policy and for wage adjustment policy, of regulating wages according to measured changes in output per worker or according to some other formula that might be considered desirable.

George P. Schultz and Robert Z. Aliber (eds.), *Guidelines: Informal Controls and the Market Place* (Chicago: The University of Chicago Press, 1966), plus a spate of literature on wage-price relationships cited in conjunction with the wage level criteria discussion of Chapter 7.

The micro rule of wages adjusted, market by market, in conformance with the relative degree of labor surplus (shortage) existing in each case is attractive also. It promises reasonable adherence of wage patterns to the ebb and flow of the demand for labor relative to its supply in the different sectors of the economy.

The proposition that the degree of labor surplus or shortage existing in the various areas of the economy should guide wage pattern adjustments also is not new, is controversial, and requires investigation. Abba Lerner is an early and able proponent of the surplus-shortage idea, but others also have contributed materially to the literature on the subject. The idea is still in its infancy, and it has yet to be demonstrated that a regulation program based upon such a principle is at all feasible. This matter is discussed in Part II. But the history of the proposition deserves a note, and the writing of Henry Simons seems a natural starting point.

Simons hinted at the possibility of establishing suitable criteria for direct controls on wages based upon the market guidance (surplus-shortage) principle as early as 1941.[3] The Simons context, of course, was different from the present one for he was concerned with how to judge the amount and character of wage inequities associated with the trade union movement. Yet in the course of this investigation Simons developed criteria that also might serve as a useful guide to the establishment of a system of wage rates compatible with a competitive economic environment and with price stabilizing monetary and fiscal policy.

What Simons suggested, in essence, was that the dictates of the market would be met best if freedom of entry to new trades was preserved. In the Simons view ideal wage policy, ". . . whether for a democratic capitalism or for a democratic socialism. . ."[4] ought to be constructed upon this principle. He suggested that:[5]

> Freedom of migration implies freedom of qualified workers, not merely to seek jobs but to get them; free entry implies full employment for all qualified persons who wish to enter. Whether the wage permits an adequate family scale of living, according to social service workers, is simply irrelevant—as, indeed, are the net earnings of employers. What really mat-

3. Publication of these remarks appeared a few years later. Henry Simons, "Some Reflections on Syndicalism," *Journal of Political Economy*, March, 1944, esp. pp. 14-19.
4. *Ibid.*, p. 14.
5. *Ibid.*

ters is the judgment of workers who would be excluded by an excessive wage as to the *relative* merits of the employment alternatives actually open to them. Other things equal, the wage is too high if higher than the wage in actually alternative employments. Ethically, one cannot go beyond the opinion of qualified workers seeking to transfer. If in large numbers they prefer employment here to the alternatives and cannot get it, the wage is excessive.

J. M. Clark is another who advocated the "market" guide at a comparatively early date.[6] The Clark contribution also is significant in at least two other respects. The Clark context, unlike that of Simons, is quite similar to the present one, for Clark was concerned both with "too high" wages and with "inappropriate" wage patterns, which he believed to be undesirable side effects of collective bargaining by strong unions. Further, Clark's analysis is in some detail and the remedy suggested is establishment of wage codes ". . . based on facts and reason, not on a mere test of strength."[7]

Clark extended beyond the scope and context of Simons when he suggested in detail how and why[8]

> . . . individual industries' hourly wage scales should, over, let us say, a ten-year period, rise as much as the average increase in man-hour productivity for the whole economy, and no more, except as may be necessary to rectify inequities between trades and industries. This leaves room for an upward bias, since the adjustments of inequities would be prevailing upward; and this would presumably cause the total wage structure to exceed the original average standard; but it should be possible to keep this excess within the bounds of tolerable price inflation, already discussed. With experience, it should be possible to do better than this, by learning how much this upward bias amounts to, and making some allowance for it in setting the original over-all yearly rate of increase which is taken as a point of departure.

Harry Henig also worked with the idea of using market employment data to guide wage rate adjustment at an early date.[9] Henig's

6. *Guideposts in Time of Change* (New York: Harper and Bros., 1949), esp. pp. 147-78; reprinted with permission.

7. *Ibid.*, p. 188.

8. *Ibid.*, p. 175.

9. "A Functional Criterion for Wage Appraisal," *Journal of Political Economy*, February, 1952, pp. 44-60. A reference to this criterion is also found

approach was the Simons one of attempting to evaluate the magnitude of monopoly influences in the labor market; and he specifically rejected both Clark's productivity criterion as a guide to wage level determination and Clark's suggestion for general controls on wages. However, Henig went well beyond Simons and Clark, in a manner parallel with Lerner,[10] in the analysis of how and why a measured labor surplus (shortage) might be used to appraise the economic effectiveness of a given labor market.

In England a number of economists have made contributions, most notably James Meade. As early as 1949 Meade referred to the possibility of wage controls with an anti-inflation purpose and commented upon the desirability of using labor market employment data to guide market by market adjustment in relative wages under such conditions.[11] Later, in his *Control of Inflation*, Meade repeated and expanded upon these ideas somewhat.[12]

Nonetheless, a primary contribution, if not the primary contribution, must certainly be said to have come from Abba Lerner. Lerner's major work on the subject was published at the comparatively early date of 1952, and this work owes a debt to some of his earlier publications.[13] Lerner's writings clearly underlie a number

---

in S. Herbert Unterberger and Harry Henig, "Theory of the Wage Control in the Transition Period," *Southern Economic Journal*, January, 1946, esp. p. 287.

10. *Economics of Employment*, pp. 191-241.

11. *Planning and the Price Mechanism* (New York: The Macmillan Co., 1949), p. 76.

12. *The Control of Inflation* (Cambridge: Cambridge University Press, 1958).

13. Lerner has made more than one suggestion for inflation control. The proposal referred to here and throughout this book is perhaps his best known, i.e., wage controls as a companion policy to price stabilizing monetary and fiscal policy. This suggestion is described in his *Economics of Employment*.

However, Lerner's proposal for wage controls enjoys a number of similarities with the 1944 "rule" of welfare developed in his doctoral dissertation and later published as *The Economics of Control* (New York: The Macmillan Company, 1944).

The primary objective of *The Economics of Control* seems to have been to develop a general set of criteria for the operation of a socialistic state that would at one and the same time capitalize upon what Lerner obviously considers a prime advantage of a free enterprise system, that of free consumer choice, and also eliminate what he considers capitalism's most serious defect, unregulated monopoly. This dual objective, according to Lerner, is accomplished by his welfare "rule." Lerner's proposal for wage regulation as a means of inflation control is similar to his 1944 "rule" in that it too attempts to allow free consumer choice while seeking to contain an "evil" of free capitalistic systems, in this case cost inflation.

of the more recent excursions into the area of wage controls as an anti-inflationary device, most notably the President's guideposts to non-inflationary wage and price bargaining. Lerner's work on wage controls, which is somewhat incidental to his main purpose and therefore not impressively long, even today seems well reasoned and comparatively detailed. Lerner would not claim to have conquered all the problems facing a program of the sort which he proposes, but his analysis goes much beyond mere suggestion that wage controls, properly structured, might provide an effective aid to inflation control. He proposes specific control criteria that he believes to be workable or capable of being made workable. Hence the review of his proposal that follows should indicate some of the strengths and weaknesses of the idea.

THE LERNER PROPOSAL

The Lerner idea for inflation control consists of a two-pronged approach to the inflation problem. As an attack upon demand inflation, when it occurs, Lerner proposes what he calls functional finance. This is price stabilizing monetary and fiscal policy. This part of the Lerner proposal, too, is controversial. It is examined in Chapter 6. As an attack upon cost inflation, Lerner suggests direct controls on wages.

As Lerner explains it, excessive bargaining power of labor and wage rigidities are significant causes of inflation. Hence, neutralization of these causes becomes an important policy objective. In the view of Lerner this best might be accomplished by imposition of general wage controls as a companion to monetary and fiscal policy. In this way, it is contended, inflation can be eliminated while unemployment is kept at the irreducible level of frictional unemployment only, so that Lerner's high full employment becomes an achievable objective even given the need to maintain price-level stability.

Satisfactory wage policy has several requisites. Lerner believes that wage policy must be directed at specific wage rates in particular markets. While control of the aggregate wage bill ought to be the prime objective of wage policy, wage controls also should permit optimum resource allocation. Since changes in the structure and composition of the economy are inevitable, any regulatory scheme must permit the wage pattern to shift with structural adjustments. Otherwise unemployment will be the consequence of price stabilizing monetary and fiscal policy.[14]

As Lerner sees it, the only way to regulate wages to conform properly to shifts in productivity and demand structure is by means of adjustments in individual wage rates. It is important that the essentially free character of economic markets be maintained.[15]

> In a free society, the workers can be obtained only by making the conditions of work and the pay sufficiently attractive to induce them to move to the places where they are needed or by making the conditions of work and the pay sufficiently bad where they are not needed to induce the proper number of workers to leave these places and go elsewhere. The final judges in a free society must be the workers themselves, free to move or not to move in accordance with their own judgment of the adequacy of the pay and of the attractiveness of the conditions of work.

In other words, when the important social function which wages perform is recognized (*i.e.*, wage differentials help induce labor or factor mobility) it is clear that wage rates must fluctuate in response to changing market conditions.

To determine what relative wage rates should be, Lerner advocates the use of "indices of relative attractiveness." These would be calculated both for the nation and for individual labor markets. The "national average index" would be the ratio of unemployed members of the work force to employed workers. The index for a particular market would be the ratio of workers qualified and ready to work but not engaged in an area, to the workers employed in the area. Lerner then proposes that where the national average index exceeds that of a particular area, wages in the area should rise, and conversely.

Lerner's formula requires that percentage changes in wages vary with national productivity increases and with the percentage difference between the national average index and the area index of relative attractiveness. However, the Lerner formula does not call for absolute decreases in wages under any circumstances. As Lerner explains:[16]

---

14. It would, of course, be possible to adjust to a trend change in the value of money if this should be the goal selected.

15. *Economics of Employment*, pp. 213-14; reprinted with permission.

16. *Ibid.*, p. 215.

Where the index of relative attractiveness is more than twice the national average, the money wage rate should not be raised at all but should be kept constant while other wages move ahead. . . . Where the index of relative attractiveness is not too different from the national average, say between half the national average and double the national average, the money wage should be increased at 3 per cent per annum, that being an approximation to the long-run increase in over-all productivity. . . . Where the index of relative attractiveness is less than half the national average, the wage rate should be increased at twice the standard rate, i.e., at 6 per cent per annum.

Under the Lerner criteria, areas of relative labor surplus would experience relative wage decreases and areas of relative labor shortage relative wage increases. Individual wage rates would depend upon the eagerness of workers to move into or out of a specific area, industry, or job classification, combined with the intensity of the need of employers for workers in the various area, industry and skill classifications. General wage level adjustments would be tied to national average improvements in the productivity, output per worker, of labor.

Lerner is optimistic about the possibility of overcoming any difficulties in administration of his proposal, a key issue. Lerner argues that his wage policy proposal need not be administered by any arbitrary authority.[17] He expresses the belief that workers, management, and the public should be capable of making their own calculations, provided only that the considerable quantity of necessary statistical data be readily available. Lerner suggests that it might be helpful to establish "regional committees" to function as central depositories for statistical data and to assist interested parties in making the necessary calculations. The regional committees, however, would not need any enforcement powers. The pressure of public opinion supposedly would be sufficient to induce most recalcitrant groups to conform to the established standard.

Lerner further contends that his "steering wheel" adjustment process, by which wage policy decisions are reached through a process of successive approximation, would facilitate the regulatory process greatly. Elaborate forecasts of future labor market trends and of the consequences of particular policy actions would not be

17. *Ibid.*, p. 216.

necessary. Neither would detailed analysis of such issues as wage justice. Instead, any wage decisions would be provisional only and could be amended by experience.

CONCLUSION

There seems to be a growing belief among economists that some sort of national wages policy is both desirable and practicable. But the theoretical basis for such a belief is scanty. It needs to be strengthened if such a judgment is to have real economic content and meaning.

Given some variant of wage-push inflation, a national incomes policy program—which is dependent upon price-stabilizing monetary and fiscal arrangements for maintenance of the general level of aggregate monetary demand, and which concentrates upon insuring compatible wage adjustments—has a good deal of logic in its favor. It is not the only possible wage control program with an anti inflation intent that might be developed. However, under the assumption that wage inflation and demand inflation pressures often exist side-by-side, such a program seems to offer the greatest chance of success. Its adoption allows for a continuance of monetary and fiscal policies in their now customary roles of adjusting the general level of aggregate demand, although there would be some departure in rules of application. In the future the goal of price-level stabilization would become the chief objective rather than one of several objectives that monetary and fiscal policy was expected to accomplish. Its adoption also allows for the development of a wage policy designed to foster the objectives of a market directed economy operating under reasonably competitive conditions. It assures that regulation of the general wage level and regulation of wage patterns be in accord with the relative supply of and demand for labor in aggregate and marked by market.

This does not say that a national incomes policy program used in conjunction with the more orthodox tools of monetary and fiscal policy offers sure success. The ability successfully to direct a co-ordinated monetary and fiscal policy program toward the stated goal of price-level stabilization is controversial, and the impact which wage policy would have on monetary and fiscal arrangements so directed is not clear. Hence, this aspect of the control program outlined needs further study. Beyond this there is considerable doubt as to which specific control criteria, out of the many possible, offer the greatest chance of success. Indeed, it is most uncertain that any set of criteria is sufficiently promising to warrant its use in an actual situation.

It has been suggested that if private bargaining over wages is to be regulated, the selected control criteria should follow the same principles that guide the unregulated, competitive market. Control criteria have been proposed to adjust the level of wages in accord with measured changes in output per worker and relative wages with relative labor surpluses (shortages) market by market. But, the output per worker formula is controversial. The surplus-shortage guide, while theoretically correct for a competitive economy, may not be the wisest choice under conditions of regulation. Problems of implementation, while rarely mentioned or treated in detail by professional economists, need significant consideration. After all, economists long have been aware of criteria which if applied faithfully would improve immeasurably the workings of any economy. The problem usually is one of implementation. Were it not for this issue, socialism might be the universally accepted solution.

Chapter 6

WAGE POLICY AND STABILIZATION POLICY

UNDERLYING THE ANTI-INFLATION PROPOSAL which this book is designed to investigate is the assumption that price stabilizing monetary and fiscal policy can be employed effectively to eliminate price-level fluctuations[1] and that such a program would not be affected adversely by the wage policy developed. Both these propositions are controversial. They require further examination.

As this chapter will attempt to demonstrate, not only are obstacles to stabilization of the price-level through monetary and fiscal policy very great indeed but price stabilizing monetary and fiscal policy cannot be considered independently of wage policy. It is unlikely, given the pattern of wages and given unregulated product markets, that more than one total wage bill for the nation is fully compatible with a given level of prices. Whatever wage policy is adopted undoubtedly will affect the ease and speed with which monetary and fiscal policy is able to cope with inappropriate levels of aggregate monetary demand. Wage policy may affect even the possibility of adjustment. Moreover, the specific price-level objectives set for monetary and fiscal policy and the speed with which these objectives are achieved undoubtedly will affect the success of whatever wage policy is developed.

---

1. Of course, according to wage-push theorists, monetary and fiscal policy structured in this way would result in an unacceptable level of unemployment. But this fact, at best, has a modest bearing upon the hypothetical question, could the general price-level be stabilized?

Stated in slightly different terms, the interdependence of micro-economic and macro-economic wage policy as well as the interdependence of wage policy and the general economic environment is a recurring theme of this work. Because of this interdependence, the way in which policies in one sector are structured and the success achieved in their implementation bear directly upon the difficulty of achieving success in some other sector.

THE ROLE OF PRICE-STABILIZING MONETARY AND FISCAL POLICY

In an effort to assess the efficacy of price-stabilizing monetary and fiscal policy, the problems which give rise to the considerable dispute among monetary theorists as to whether rules are preferable to discretionary authority are illuminating, as they serve to point up some of the considerable difficulties in the price stabilization task. And, it might be added that arguments similar to those developed concerning monetary policy could also be presented with fiscal policy as the example, as there is a close similarity between the two cases.[2]

Insofar as monetary policy is concerned, in the rules versus discretion debate, the question of which control format is ideal or nearly ideal is not at issue. Rather the controversy centers on which is least objectionable. Discretionary policy is difficult to administer because ability to predict economic trends is inadequate, as is ability to predict the impact of particular monetary and fiscal policy changes. It is impossible to forecast precisely either the amplitude or the timing of fluctuations in general economic activity. Even if accurate predictions were possible, discretionary policy would suffer from lack of adequate criteria for determining either the proper timing or the proper magnitude of corrective policy.[3]

Some economists, notably Professor Friedman, also contend

2. See, for example, A. W. Phillips, "Stabilization Policy in a Closed Economy," *Economic Journal,* June, 1954, pp. 290-323; and "Stabilization Policy and the Time-Forms of Lagged Response," *Economic Journal*, June, 1957, pp. 265-77; W. J. Baumol, "Pitfalls in Contracyclical Policies: Some Tools and Results," *The Review of Economics and Statistics*, February 1961, pp. 21-26; and D. J. Smith, "Can Automatic Stabilizers be Destabilizing?" *Public Finance*, 1963, pp. 357-63.

3. Again note the parallel with fiscal policy. John Cornwall, for one, shows that the main fiscal policy problems center on the time path of adjustment to a target level of income and on the magnitude of fiscal policy change

that an allowance for discretionary authority lacks a check on the sincerity of intent of the monetary authority. And, here too there exists a parallel with fiscal policy. As Friedman explains it, in either inflation or deflation it cannot be determined with certainty whether the price movement is due to wavering administrative intent or to an error in judgment.

But rules for monetary policy action aimed at price stability also suffer from serious inadequacies. The Mints rule which would have the monetary authority begin to take corrective action if his selected index of measured prices rose above 103 or fell below 97, for example, permits considerable latitude for judgment.[4] How much corrective action should be taken under the rule, and how quickly implemented? Problems of error in forecasting economic trends and policy effects are not avoided through use of a rule for monetary policy action of this sort.

For these and other reasons, Friedman and his fellows advocate stabilizing the supply of money, with allowance for secular increases in the demand for money. But stabilization of the supply of money is a compromise solution. In effect proponents of this rule admit that controls powerful enough to regulate the economy now exist, but deny that economists have the wisdom to know when and in what degree to employ them. Even if economists were so knowledgeable, Friedman and his followers suspect that policy mistakes still would be common because the influence of economists on administrative decisions is far from total. Hence there are also serious compromises with the ideal in the suggestion that discretionary policy be abandoned, that the economy be required to suffer whatever fluctuations ensue, and that a certain amount of price-level fluctuation be accepted as inevitable.

Beyond the above, the proposal that prices guide policy action raises the question whether stabilization of measured prices is an appropriate goal, and which index ought to be stabilized. Dispute as to the appropriateness of maintaining the general price-level often centers on whether price-level stability and full capacity-full employment levels of economic activity are compatible objectives. Such an objection is inappropriate at this point. Wage-push theorists specifically contend that high employment and price-level

needed to yield the target level. "The Structure of Fiscal Models," *Quarterly Journal of Economics*, November, 1965, pp. 608-22.

4. Lloyd W. Mints, *Monetary Policy for a Competitive Society.*

stability now are not fully compatible, and that other means, *e.g.*, direct controls, must be developed to cope with this aspect of the problem.

On the other hand, objections to stabilization of measured prices may rest on the doubt that any one index constitutes a satisfactory policy guide. This is a substantive issue. Essentially there are three broad stabilization possibilities: stabilization of some indexes of wages, of intermediate product prices, or of prices of final products. In evaluating the relative merits of possible courses of action, it is necessary to consider the impact of inflation that policy is supposed to control,[5] and the degree to which available indexes meet certain elaborate statistical requirements.

Stabilization of the level of final product prices is the most orthodox of price stabilization goals. It is the goal selected for study by this work. The customary argument is that stabilization of final product prices fosters a desirable level of economic activity and permits development of the most equitable pattern of income distribution. By contrast, stabilization of wholesale prices would be associated with falling retail prices, and therefore recession, as well as wage rate increases averaging less than labor's increases in productivity. Typically it would be objected to for these reasons. Stabilization of money wages is objected to even more strongly than stabilization of wholesale prices, for wage level stabilization would be associated with retail prices falling more sharply, and recessionary tendencies more intense, than if wholesale prices were stabilized.

From the standpoint of the impact of inflation to be controlled, then, stabilization of final product prices is the usual goal. Objections to this approach most often center on the relative statistical merits of available indexes together with the qualifying remark that the primary objective is to stabilize some prices and that, from the standpoint of impact on output and/or distributive shares, the question of which prices is relatively unimportant. A really fundamental problem is that, for present purposes, the requirements of a good index are elaborate and difficult if not impossible to meet.

The index should be broadly based to reflect accurately general economic activity. For the same reason it should include considera-

5. Clearly there is some tie-in here with the discussion in Part I of the relationship between inflation cause and impact.

tion of the variety and relative importance of investment goods and of governmental purchases as well as consumer purchases. Prices stabilized ought to be sensitive to changing economic conditions, but not subject to wild fluctuations, so that the signal for corrective policy is adequately prompt and accurate, but is not over-drawn. Prices which do not move freely and independently, such as those supported by government action, should be excluded from consideration to further aid sensitivity of the index. Undue attention to insignificant products should be avoided as a time-saving device.

All this suggests that the index selected will have a direct bearing upon the character of the results obtained from implementation of a wage control program with an anti-inflation intent. It suggests further that no existing index is likely to be as useful for such purposes as one that might be constructed. More than this, the critics of the wage control proposal which this book examines here have placed their fingers on an important weakness. Obtainable statistical data may not be adequate for so elaborate and formal a regulatory process as that contemplated.

As a second objection, sometimes it is argued that attempts to stabilize a particular price index would be economically de-stabilizing on balance rather than stabilizing. Such an activity might be destabilizing in its impact on the economy for reasons of error of forecast of future price-level movements. It also might fail to stabilize the economy because of error of forecast of the impact, timing, or magnitude of corrective policy action. The period multiplier phenomenon is one explanation as to why this might be so. Accelerator effects comprise another explanation. But of primary importance is the presence of spending lags. Because of all of these difficulties, attempts at regulation of the economy within too narrow limits actually can cause fluctuations rather than smooth them out.

In summary a number of obstacles combine to reduce the effectiveness of monetary and fiscal policy aimed at measured price-level stabilization. The effectiveness of price stabilizing monetary and fiscal policy is determined by the speed and accuracy of measurement of cyclical fluctuations, by ability to forecast the future, by the manner in which various sectors of the economy respond to monetary and fiscal policy changes, and by ability to predict this response. Because of failings in these areas, it is quite possible that a national incomes policy to assist in the control of wage inflation would break down, not because the incomes policy as such was at fault, but because cooperating policies upon which the control proposal depends are not sufficiently advanced to be reliable in this context.

WAGE POLICY AND STABILIZATION POLICY

Price stabilizing monetary and fiscal policy is fraught with complexities and uncertainties, and we must rid ourselves of any idea that wage policy may be independent of price stabilization policy. One of the larger and more significant areas of response to price stabilizing monetary and fiscal policy undoubtedly is that of the wage sector. This means that the form and character of adjustments by the wages sector to monetary and fiscal policy is crucial to aggregative economic administration. Keynes recognized this fact in his discussion of the nature of the employment function.[6] And the treatment which this issue has received in the literature following the *General Theory* underscores the importance of the relationship.

Today the danger is in forgetting that now customary assumptions about the behavior of the wage sector: that money wages (and other costs) evidence considerable downward rigidity, and rise but slowly in the face of excess aggregate monetary demand at least until a position of full or near full employment is reached, are just that—assumptions. But they are exceedingly important. One of the primary conclusions of the Keynesian model is that monetary and/or fiscal policy is an effective means of regulating levels of output and employment. This conclusion has been so thoroughly strengthened by subsequent excursions into the area of applied macroeconomic theory that it now seems in the category of an economic axiom.

But suppose the Keynesian assumptions about the behavior of wages in response to a change in aggregate demand no longer held true. Suppose instead that the general level of wages were to move simultaneously and proportionately with changes in total spending, or that the general level of wages lagged behind changes in total spending only very slightly. Under these conditions the conclusions of the Keynesian model, indeed of much thinking in macro-eco-

6. *The General Theory of Employment, Interest, and Money,* pp. 280-91.

nomic theory, would not apply. The response of the economy to monetary and fiscal policy would differ in timing and magnitude, and perhaps also direction, from what has been the experience in the past. This is because the effects of macro-economic policy on levels of employment and output are allied closely to the ability of policy to affect the real wage. If this ability changes, so do the results of policy action.

Caution must be used when a Keynesian type aggregative analysis is employed in which the policy tool for dealing with either inflation or deflation is price stabilizing monetary and fiscal policy, if at the same time the entire character of the wage determination process is to be changed. One way to demonstrate this point is to describe some wage control criteria which would interfere with stabilization efforts of monetary and fiscal policy, orthodoxly managed.

A wage policy would be quite disruptive under which the level of wages shifted simultaneously, but several fold more than proportionately, with a change in monetary and/or fiscal policy. Price-level stability would be difficult to achieve through monetary and fiscal policy because of the promptness and inappropriateness of the response of the wage sector. The average level of employment which occurred under these conditions would be disappointing because average wages would bear so little relation to the supply of labor relative to the demand for it.

As a second example, a wage policy which subjected wages to frequent, violent and random change also would interfere with price stabilizing monetary and fiscal policy. Such a wage policy would further detract from both the stability and predictability of the economic system. As a final example of destabilizing wage policy, wages could be adjusted to offset monetary and fiscal policy. This could render the latter sterile as a policy device.

Wage policy could be destabilizing. Hence, the danger is present that a national incomes policy program with an anti wage inflation purpose might be destabilizing rather than stabilizing. Indeed, several factors point to this result. An underlying principle of any national incomes policy that might be developed is likely to be that national wage level adjustments should coincide as nearly as possible with changes in aggregate monetary demand. But if this objective is to be accomplished at all well, wage policy will be destabilizing if it is not qualitatively appropriate. Moreover, if contrasts between the immediate and the longer term effects of wage changes resulting from a change in monetary and fiscal policy are not taken into account when planning monetary and fiscal policy moves, then, again, the wage policy program adopted may exert a destabilizing influence.

The relationship between wage policy and monetary and fiscal policy also works the other way. The degree to which monetary and fiscal policy is able to stabilize the price-level and spending in various sectors of the economy will affect the difficulty of the wage administration task. Macro-economic policy which results in a need for frequent and violent changes in wage policy makes the task of wage administration more difficult, makes it less likely that the developed wage policy will properly complement monetary and fiscal policy, and lessens the chances that monetary and fiscal policy will be able effectively to stabilize the level of prices.

CONCLUSION

Monetary and fiscal policy aimed at stabilization of some index of measured prices is an inaccurate policy device. Some economists even question whether it could be successful enough in achieving economic stability to warrant its use. Should monetary and fiscal policy be employed as a stabilization device its limitations are certain to complicate the task of wage administration, but the intensity of these complications will be affected greatly by the way in which the monetary and fiscal policy program is organized and administered. The facility with which policy makers adjust their fiscal instruments is important, but so is the price-level index to be stabilized and the degree of stabilization to be attempted.

Not only is the adequacy of monetary and fiscal policy going to affect wage policy problems, but wage policy will affect the results to be obtained from a given set of monetary and fiscal adjustments. Administered wages could facilitate general stabilization efforts or so complicate them as to vitiate both price stabilizing monetary and fiscal arrangements and national incomes policy; it would depend upon the particular guidelines set forth.

It is evident that whatever incomes policy program is developed will have to consider the needs of stabilization policy, and the effectiveness of stabilization policy will have to be considered when deciding if an incomes policy would be useful as an anti-inflationary device.

Chapter 7

WAGE LEVEL CRITERIA

REGULATION OF THE TOTAL WAGE BILL is the *raison d'être* for national incomes policy as an inflation deterrent. But the anti-inflation objective is designed to be accomplished by influencing individual wage settlements in individual markets in such a way that the total of all wages paid is economically satisfactory.[1] In a sense, then, establishment of the wage bill should be regarded as a micro-economic problem because whether or not the government can bring about desired changes in the general level of wages depends upon the degree of success it can achieve in influencing particular wages in particular markets.

In spite of this, it is the contention of this work that discussion of macro-economic criteria for wage determination is more than justified. The reasons are several: (1) Imperfections that exist in the practical criteria for micro-economic wage adjustment which are available necessitate a macro-economic guide in addition to a micro-economic guide to wage adjustments. (2) Several criteria are available that might provide a workable guide to macro-economic wage adjustments. (3) Choice among these guides is difficult, for they all have serious drawbacks. (4) Certainly there is no evidence to indicate that measured changes in output per worker over the nation would be noticeably superior to other macro-economic wage guides available.

1. Definition of a wage is a complex task as it must include some consideration of fringe benefits and basis of payment. These problems are discussed in Chapter 10.

70

These propositions and reasons need investigation, obviously. Preliminary to this discussion, however, it is necessary to examine some more fundamental points. What are the essential characteristics of an appropriate macro-economic wage? What are the chief problems of macro-economic wage regulation? Do these difficulties seem surmountable?

PRELIMINARY ISSUES

Chapter 5 listed several objectives for a national incomes policy, if it is successfully to aid monetary and fiscal arrangements aimed at wage inflation control. The wage program must so complement monetary and fiscal policy as to render the latter a workable policy device, or at least it must not render monetary and fiscal policy unworkable as a means of price stabilization. The program must provide both for a reduction in the level of unemployment that the economy would experience with stable prices, and for a reduction in the secular level of unemployment regardless of the price policy pursued. The control program must also provide for mobility within and between labor markets consistent with reasonable demands of economic efficiency.

In total these requirements amount to recognition that the wage bill appropriate in a given instance depends in part upon the pattern of wages that exists, in part upon monetary and fiscal policy, and in part upon general economic conditions. Conversely, the pattern of wages that is appropriate depends upon the wage bill, upon monetary and fiscal policy, and upon general economic conditions. In other words, if wages were adjusted by government fiat, it soon should become evident that adjustments in the wage bill cannot be separated from adjustments in wage patterns, any more than wage policy can be set independently of the economic environment.

This suggests that a perfect wage regulation program, aimed at assisting monetary and fiscal policy in the control of wage inflation, must include provision for application of simultaneous equations to the regulatory process so that wage pattern changes, wage level changes, and monetary and fiscal adjustments can be concordant. Moreover, since the full effects of economic changes are not immediately communicated to the entire economy, but influence the economy at different rates in different ways over time, micro and macro wage policy as well as monetary and fiscal policy would have to be tailored to take this into account.

Clearly the above is neither possible nor necessary. A wage regulation program need not be perfect, or even nearly so, to represent a substantial improvement over present market practices. But curiously enough, inability to accomplish the ideal does have a strong implication for policy in another direction. Once the ideal is scrapped, and it is admitted that simultaneous solutions cannot be perfectly determined which meet both the needs of the present and the consequences of changing effects over time of the policy actions taken, then the possibility must be considered that anti-inflation policies could be destabilizing rather than stabilizing. Should this prove to be the case it obviously would vitiate national incomes policy in conjunction with monetary and fiscal policy for inflation control.

Chapter 6 considered several aspects of this problem: Review of the debate over rules versus discretionary authority in monetary policy pointed up the danger that price stabilizing monetary and fiscal policy might be destabilizing in its result rather than stabilizing. It was suggested in another context that wage policy also might be destabilizing rather than stabilizing, because of feedback effects on monetary and fiscal policy. Finally, destabilizing monetary and fiscal policy certainly would make the wage adjustment task more difficult, just as destabilizing wage policy would make price stabilizing monetary and fiscal policy more difficult.

These same principles apply within the wage regulation sphere. A wildly fluctuating wage level, for example, would complicate greatly the job of adjusting wage patterns, just as frequent and sweeping changes in wage patterns would complicate greatly the job of adjusting the wage level.

As an additional problem, although not discussed in Chapter 6, the symptoms of inappropriate monetary and fiscal policy and of inappropriate wage policy frequently are similar. A change in aggregate monetary demand, for example, will affect levels of employment, total wages paid, the relative share of income going to labor, and measured output per worker. Conversely, a change in wage policy has price-level implications through its effect on aggregate monetary demand. This further complicates the task of regulating wages in conjunction with price stabilizing monetary and fiscal policy.

The fact that perfection in regulation of the macro-economic wage, wage patterns, and price stabilizing monetary and fiscal policy is impossible, and that attempts to regulate more than one of these areas will result in some doubt as to the meaning of traditional signals to policy action, does not mean that regulation is impossible. It does mean that standards of administrative performance will have to be reasonable and failure in one sector of regulation may reveal itself, in part, through increased regulatory difficulties elsewhere. Regulatory formulas need to consider not just the ideal, but also how to mitigate the consequences of failures to reach perfection which are inevitable. Translated into a policy guide, this is quite likely to mean that in order to facilitate analysis of the economic problem of the moment, and to ease the task of promoting economic stability, policy adjustments probably will have to be somewhat modest in amount or infrequent. A process of successive approximation in matters of wage policy and monetary and fiscal policy by which previous policy errors are detected after the fact, and corrected through a series of compensating adjustments, will have to be used sparingly. This places an increased burden upon the administrative authority correctly to predict on the first try the direction and magnitude of necessary wage adjustments as well as monetary and fiscal adjustments.

As a further complication to macro-economic wage determination, it is doubtful if an aggregate wage target can be set in the sense that some sort of wages fund is established and divided among those employed. Instead, the approach of the Federal government surely must be occasionally to prescribe the average change in wage rates deemed desirable in light of available economic data. The total wage bill could be established directly only if the government prescribed the distribution of workers and level of employment firm by firm along with wage rates. But this would so complicate the incomes policy, developed for what in reality is little gain, that it hardly seems wise.

If the distribution and level of employment are allowed to remain independent variables to be established through traditional interplay of market forces, then adjustment of the wage level, defined as equivalent to an average change in wages, will have an uncertain effect upon the total of wages paid. This leads to an obvious difficulty. If, for example, the wage bill is assumed to be too low, is it because the wage level is too low, or too high?

Stated in somewhat different terms, the wage bill cannot be set directly when the pattern and level of employment are not under direct control. Hence, the more interesting policy questions center not on the probable consequences of setting an economically incorrect wage bill, but on the consequences of *attempting* to set an economically incorrect wage bill. For this reason it is best to view the concept of a "too high" or a "too low" wage bill in the planned rather than the realized sense, or else to employ what is perhaps the more usual approach and talk in terms of desired changes in the wage level or average changes in wages.

To place the wage policy task in perspective, then, comparison with the ideal is not particularly meaningful. Instead, the appropriate administrative benchmark ought to be the less ambitious one that performance should be better than for the uncontrolled market. But this has consequences not only for what is acceptable, but for administrative procedures that ought to be employed.

Of course, the fact that market determined wage levels and wage patterns are imperfect and that, therefore, standards of performance for regulated wages ought to be lower than they otherwise would be, does not mean that opportunity for improvement beyond the necessary minimum should be ignored. An efficient job of wage regulation is desirable because it leads to greater economic achievement. More than this, the way in which national incomes policy procedures are structured and the degree of success in their administration have a direct bearing upon the success of economic administration elsewhere, as, for example, the success of monetary and fiscal policy aimed at price-level stabilization. Even within the broad category of wage administration, the way in which one set of problems is handled affects the degree of success that will be achieved in the handling of other problems. Ineptitude in the selection of macro-economic goals, for example, will complicate wage judgments on the micro-economic level, and conversely.

To conclude, discussion of preliminary issues should have elicited several general points relevant to the problem of determining an appropriate macro-economic wage. Micro-economic and macro-economic wage policy are closely interrelated, as are wage policies and the general economic environment. To be effective, macro-economic wage policy must be in accord with other economic policies and with the particular institutional setting. The need for accord implies that inappropriate wage policy may provide regulatory problems elsewhere in the economy, and that failure to reach an appropriate wage level will result in compromise of important economic objectives. Finally, perfection in wage level determination is neither a realistic goal nor, necessarily, a satisfactory guide to regulatory techniques.

ALTERNATIVE CRITERIA FOR DETERMINATION OF THE WAGE BILL

Several points have been made which now require discussion: (1) Imperfections that exist in the practical criteria for micro-economic wage adjustment which are available necessitate a macro-economic guide in addition to a micro-economic guide to wage adjustments. (2) Several criteria are available that might provide a workable guide to macro-economic wage adjustments. (3) Choice among these guides is difficult, for they all have serious drawbacks. (4) Certainly there is no evidence to indicate that measured changes in output per worker over the nation would be noticeably superior to other macro-economic wage guides available. Investigation of marginal productivity theory is a useful starting point for investigation of these propositions.

Marginal Productivity as an Adjustment Criterion. A common theoretical approach to wage determination on the micro-economic level is marginal productivity analysis. Undoubtedly marginal productivity theory does have substantial relevance for most labor markets. It is a useful micro-economic generalization. Often it accurately describes how wages are established. Further, it contains implications for how wages best might be established.

The marginal productivity principle also has macro-economic implications. Regardless of the form which the theory takes, and the possibilities are several although they usually differ in their inclusiveness,[2] marginal productivity theory is a wage theory for the economy as a whole.[3] For the individual firm it is a theory

2. See, for example, Allan Cartter, *Theory of Wages and Employment* (Homewood: Richard D. Irwin, Inc., 1959), esp. pp. 11-32.

3. This is not to say that traditional versions of marginal productivity theory accurately reflect real world situations, for they may not. The fact that these theories must assume firms price at the low point on their average total cost curves or else experience constant returns to scale (the mathematician's typical requirement of a homogenous linear production function of the first

of employment, which is tantamount to saying that on the micro-
level it is a theory of relative wages.

In other words, it is possible to conceive of a supply of labor
schedule (supply of capital schedule) in aggregate which is the
summation of individual market cases. Such a concept of an aggregate supply curve of labor is a cumbersome one, of course. Especially troublesome is the fact that labor is not a homogenous
product. Since patterns of employment shift with wage level changes
and with the reason for wage level changes, this means that implicit
in any aggregate labor supply curve are assumptions about employment patterns. But, while theoretical problems involved in making
summations necessary to the construct of an aggregate labor supply
curve are more difficult than for a supply curve facing an industry
or firm, there is no reason to assume these problems are any more
difficult than those associated with other macro-economic con-
structs now in common use. In other words, the concept of an
aggregate labor supply curve involves fundamental problems of
aggregation which have for a long time troubled macro-economic
theorists.[4]

If, then, one proceeds to construct a supply of labor schedule
(supply of capital schedule), it is possible to derive a labor/output
(capital/output) ratio and a theory of the level of wages (profits),
based on the economic value of incremental increases in the work
force (stock of capital) matched against the cost of the increases.
All this is significant on two levels.

On one level, if marginal productivity theory were applied
strictly in every market situation, and if this were presumed to yield
economically satisfactory results on that level, then by summation
a correct macro-economic wage would be the essential derivative.
Under these assumptions no macro-economic target would be
needed other than application of marginal productivity theory in
each and every individual market situation.

But, as is shown in Chapter 8, direct market by market application of marginal productivity theory is not administratively
feasible. Moreover, the single acceptable alternative, Abba Lerner's

---

degree) is but one feature which limits the universality of their application.
However, usual formulations of marginal productivity theory are logically
consistent, and, given the assumptions upon which the theory is founded, for
the economy as a whole it constitutes a general theory of wages.

4. For a discussion of these problems, see, for example, Gardner Ackley,
Macroeconomic Theory, pp. 570-80.

surplus-shortage criterion or something similar to it in principle of operation, can establish relative wage rates only within the context of a given wage level. This requires a macro target, and it requires one that somehow balances between the need for frequent adjustment of the wage level to conform to changing wage patterns and changing cyclical requirements and the need for infrequent adjustment of the wage level to conform to the needs of price stabilizing monetary and fiscal policy and of wage pattern determination.

On a second level, however, even if marginal productivity theory were not strictly applied in every market situation, it still might be relevant to questions of macro-economic wage policy. If marginal productivity theory provides an acceptable goal for determination of relative wage rates, and Chapter 8 assumes that it does, then to the degree that the goal is approximated on that level, marginal productivity theory provides a guide to the general wage level.

But while marginal productivity theory may lead to a theoretically acceptable aggregate wage, accumulation of data and measurement of all factors necessary to apply the theory is an unreasonable policy goal. Also there is the already mentioned danger of possible conflict with stabilization policy. Thus the questions become: What are alternate guides to wage level determination? How well might these alternates be expected to function? Four criteria will be examined in the order in which they seem most closely to approximate the marginal productivity optimum: (1) adjustment according to supply and demand, (2) relative shares as an adjustment criterion, (3) adjustment according to productivity change, and (4) adjustment in response to political or social pressures.

Adjustment According to Supply and Demand. One possible criterion upon which to base suggested changes in the wage bill would involve regulation of the level of wages so as to bring the supply of labor into equilibrium with the demand for it. This comes very close to marginal productivity theory in principle of operation, but the administrative technique is somewhat different. Instead of statistical description of marginal revenue product and labor supply schedules for the whole economy and definition of the "correct" macro-economic wage as the intercept of these two schedules, the supply and demand approach would require policy makers to base recommended wage level adjustments upon an examination of employment data. Under the supply and demand approach ideas concerning the "correct" wage level could be verified only through a process of successive approximation whereby the wage level recommendations were adjusted until the desired employment goal was achieved. A primary distinction, then, between the two techniques of wage level determination is that one (marginal productivity theory) defines an equilibrium wage directly, while the other (supply and demand principle) defines an equilibrium wage indirectly by noting the level of employment consistent with an equilibrium wage.

Fundamental to application of the supply and demand guide to wage level determination is the supposition that the aggregate supply curve of labor is upsloping, and the demand for labor is downsloping.

In the unlikely case that the supply curve of labor is backward bending, rather than downsloping throughout its length, the quantity of labor supplied and the level of wages could be inversely related. In this case a rise in the wage level might mean voluntary quits at the same time that employers no longer found it profitable to employ so many workers. Whether voluntary or involuntary unemployment then signaled too high wages, with no change in the level of prices assumed, would depend upon whether voluntary quits exceeded the decline in the quantity of labor demanded. Under these same assumptions, a fall in the wage rate would result in an increase in the number of workers offering their services, instead of a decrease. Here the symptom of a too low wage rate would be a rise rather than a decline in output and employment. The problem, in this instance, is of course complicated further by the fact that the above statements are true only for the lower reaches of the labor supply curve. In its upper reaches it would follow the more orthodox pattern.

Even when the possibility of a backward bending supply curve of labor is disregarded, the difficulties with the supply and demand criterion are several and quite serious. Counter-cyclical monetary and fiscal policy cannot always be correct in the sense that the action taken was, or will be, price stabilizing. This is particularly the case when uncertainties concerning the impact of wage level changes on total monetary demand are considered. So, too, a wage pattern never would be completely appropriate. Further, implementation of a supply and demand criterion hinges upon development of a satisfactory definition of excessive unemployment.

A given estimate of the optimum employment goal expressed in either percentage or absolute terms would be hard to verify. Even if the selected estimate were correct at the time it was chosen, changing economic conditions quickly would destroy its reliability. In addition, once wage guidelines were in effect, usual techniques for discovering the specific level of employment, frictional unemployment, that might be considered optimum would have to be adjusted if adherence to the guidelines was, to any degree, nonvoluntary. Activities of the free market no longer would be so revealing because the market no longer would be completely free; some controls on wages would be present. Frictional unemployment usually has a special connotation. It is that level of unemployment which remains when the economy is at high employment. Frictional unemployment in this sense does not bear a necessarily close relationship to available measures of unemployment. Much unemployment tolerated in the past has been, in the view of wage-push theorists, the result of rigidities and/or of the excessive bargaining power of labor.

Aside from these problems, frictional unemployment is difficult to estimate because it is influenced by many variables. It is a function of the size and character of the work force. It is a function of the mobility of the work force. And it is a function of the need for an adaptable work force as dictated by changing product demand and technology. In short, determination of the appropriate level of employment and of the policy implications of an employment change is exceedingly complex.

An increase in the level of unemployment, for example, might reflect a changed desire on the part of workers for work. In this case, the process by which a new equilibrium is achieved should not be disturbed; rather the policy definition of full employment ought to be revised. Again, an increase in the level of unemployment might be the result of a cyclical movement in the level of business activity. This would indicate a need for compensatory spending. Both monetary and fiscal policy would be affected. Here a change in the wage level might be unwise, if the fluctuation were temporary only. Instead, the policy maker usually would want to employ such palliatives as tax relief and unemployment compensation, designed to mitigate the human consequences of the cyclical fluctuation without permanently affecting the pattern of resource allocation. As still another possibility, an increase in the level of unemployment might reflect some structural maladjustment or economic malady that would merit specifically directed legislation rather than generally directed policy measures which by their very nature would be more therapeutic than curative.

The preceding is not an exhaustive listing but illustrative. As a practical matter, changes in the level of employment, even to the extent that such changes are measurable, would be an uncertain guide to the general wage level.

Successful implementation of a supply and demand criterion for wage level determination requires knowledge of, and ability to measure, the minimum level of unemployment obtainable. It also requires an understanding of, and ability to predict, causes underlying deviations from the level of employment previously determined appropriate. Aberrations in the level of employment that result from inappropriate macro-economic wage policy should be attacked on that level. Aberrations that are the result of inappropriate monetary and fiscal policy decisions, of inappropriate wage patterns, or of ordinary fluctuations about the optimum, must be handled in some other way. This suggests a point made earlier. So complex a problem as determination and maintenance of an appropriate level of employment cannot be accomplished by any one policy. Only a combination of policies and activities directed toward the final objective, high full employment, will suffice.

The coordination of these policies is an important matter. Application of simultaneous equations has been ruled out as impractical. Equally, the search for an equilibrium set, by the method of successive approximation, involves difficulties which are likely to prove vitiating. To take but one example, assume that the sole regulatory problem is coordination of monetary and fiscal adjustments with wage level changes. But both wage level changes and monetary and fiscal adjustments will have output, employment, and price-level effects. Aggregate supply is affected because wage level changes influence cost of production. Aggregate demand is affected because wage level changes have consequences for disposable personal income and, therefore, for consumption demand. The influence of a wage change on aggregate monetary demand is, however, difficult to predict. The precise result would depend upon such factors as the elasticity of labor supply and demand in aggregate, labor's marginal propensity to consume, multiplier and accelerator effects of a spending change, and the flexibility of velocity of the circulating medium of exchange.

If both prices and employment rise, therefore, it is uncertain whether the fault is inappropriate monetary and fiscal adjustment, inappropriate wage policy, or a combination of the two. If a combination, a combination in what ratio? Clearly the causes will be obscured if both monetary and fiscal adjustments and wage level changes are frequent and varied.

There are two ways to deal with the problem. One is to accept the complication and learn to deal with it. The second is to simplify the problem by encouraging business firms and others to make wage level changes only infrequently and then somewhat simultaneously and/or to make changes gradual and predictable. If the former, and if monetary and fiscal adjustments are guided by price-level changes while wage level adjustments are guided mainly by changes in the level of unemployment, then not only is there danger that adjustments in one sector will complicate corrections in the other, but at times false signals will trigger inappropriate policy action.

A simple example will illustrate this last point. Assume a too high wage level. Assume this leads to an increase in the price-level and a reduction in unemployment. The price-level change will signal deflationary monetary and fiscal adjustments. The unemployment change will demand a wage level increase. But under the assumption of the example, neither adjustment is appropriate. The postulated difficulty was a too high wage level. Monetary and fiscal adjustments are out of place, and the corrective wage policy action is a decrease in the wage level, not an increase.

Eventually, if no other factors intervene, initial errors of policy might be correctable. Through successive adjustment, policy makers might be able to find a combination of policies which would yield the employment and price-level goals sought. But even under ideal circumstances including full compliance by business and industry with government recommendations, successive adjustment would be time consuming and potentially disruptive. It seems more logical to minimize conflict by designing wage policies so as to concentrate upon trend adjustments in wage levels and to forego efforts to achieve short-term accuracy in wage level adjustments, but this, too requires a good deal of forebearance by industry. As short term shortages and surpluses in the labor market develop, the temptation to change wage rates to match the changing labor market conditions will be very great.

In summary, regulation of the wage level according to supply and demand is theoretically accurate. At the same time it may be devoid of real economic meaning. As with many questions in economic analysis, "supply and demand" is a correct response, but empty of content unless accompanied by precise analysis and definition.[5] In this case, and leaving aside the issue of compliance, the crucial question is: Can full employment be defined adequately for wage control purposes? Can the policy maker distinguish less than full employment arising from an inappropriate level of wages and less than full employment arising from other causes?

Relative Shares as an Adjustment Criterion. A second possible guide to wage level determination is relative incomes shares. In an evaluation of this criterion and still leaving aside the issue of compliance for the time-being, there are again two questions to resolve. The first is the theoretical appropriateness of the criterion. The second concerns the issue of measurement.

Adjustment of the wage level according to data on relative shares could mean something akin to adjustment by margin productivity analysis. That is, calculation of relative shares could consider shifts in both the quality and quantity of labor and capital; and adjustment according to relative shares need not mean that relative shares, so defined, remained absolutely constant, but that they changed in a way also dictated as appropriate by marginal productivity theory. If this is the approach taken, it would be subject to the same criticisms leveled against direct application of marginal productivity theory and discussed earlier in this chapter. More often, however, the suggestion that relative income shares guide wage level determination means an attempt to keep relative shares constant. The possibility that this would yield a theoretically appropriate wage level requires examination.

The suggestion that, if possible, the aggregate wage level ought to be adjusted so as to maintain constant relative shares has at its

5. These same problems of definition are present if the supply and demand criterion is applied on the micro-economic level. The definitional questions may be posed in a slightly different way and solved differently, since markets may be compared with each other and with the total, but the essential issues are the same.

foundation any of several assumptions, express or implied: (1) Factor proportions are constant or at least not likely to change very much. (2) Factor proportions may change, but over a relevant range their supply curves are of uniform unitary elasticity in some sort of proportional sense.[6] (3) Distributive shares are based entirely or chiefly upon non-economic factors and upon historical accident. For policy purposes, therefore, present ratios may be assumed as good as any. (4) If relative shares are held constant, this will induce technological and organizational improvements of the sort needed to maintain or improve present standards of economic performance.

The first and second assumptions imply the economy functioning under its present form of organization. In the recent past, in the United States at least, relative shares may have tended to remain fairly constant. On this point there was at one time fairly strong agreement among economists that relative shares had not changed very much.[7] About ten years ago, however, the relative shares discussion was revived by Professor Robert Solow with articles in the *Review of Economics and Statistics, Economic Journal,* and *American Economic Review*.[8] The Solow articles, which of course have been unusually influential, challenge the once traditional view that relative shares have remained approximately constant over the years. The Solow view since has been supported by a number of independent tests,[9] and now is widely accepted among those involved in the study of relative income shares.

Nonetheless, Solow also was on President Kennedy's Council of

6. Concern here is with the price of labor (capital) when its supply changes *relative* to that of capital (labor). For this reason, the supply curve of interest at this point is not identical to long-run supply in the usual sense. For this reason also, the concept of unitary elasticity employed at this point varies from the usual.

7. See, for example, C. W. Cobb and Paul H. Douglas, "A Theory of Production," *American Economic Review*, Supplement, March, 1929, pp. 139-65; see also Paul H. Douglas, *The Theory of Wages* (New York: Macmillan, 1934), pp. 159-66; and J. R. Hicks, *The Theory of Wages* (London: The Macmillan Co., 1932).

8. See, for example, "The Constancy of Relative Shares," *American Economic Review*, September, 1958, pp. 618-31.

9. See, for example, John R. Moroney, "Relative Income Shares in the United States, 1922-61" (Unpublished Ph.D. dissertation, Department of Economics, Duke University, 1964), a partial survey of which is to be found in John R. Moroney, "Time-Series Elasticities of Substitution and Labor's Share in U. S. Manufacturing; the Post-War Period," *Southern Economic Journal*, April, 1966, pp. 474-83.

Economic Advisors during the formative time of wage guidepost policy development; Solow is known as a leading advocate of constant elasticity of substitution production functions for econometric analysis. In both his guidepost and his CES production function attitudes Solow would seem to be telling us that his relative shares conclusions for most problems of economic analysis are not too serious a qualification of the old constancy of relative shares idea.

Thus, in the end there may not be too much practical difference between the Solow view on the one hand and the once traditional view on constancy of relative shares on the other. Bronfenbrenner, for example, argued as late as 1960 that the high degree of constancy of relative shares must be more than coincidence, and thus that, given a free market, relative shares will continue to exhibit sufficient stability in the future as to be considered approximately constant for policy purposes.[10]

Opponents of the Bronfenbrenner view might counter by saying that the past experience of the American economy lends greater significance to the normally improbable statement that factor shares are in approximate balance for the long-run as well as the short-run. But this does not make it so. Moreover, it is also true that while relative shares have shown little tendency for secular change, this is not completely accurate. This latter observation is significant because it takes a large absolute change in relative shares to become a measurable percentage change. So, here again is a probable explanation as to why CES production functions and technical progress assumed neutral are nearly universal beginning points for all current econometric analysis, on the microeconomic level. That is, for example, if capital is increasing relative to labor,[11] then only supposition number two (above) provides an "explanation" for approximate constancy of relative shares in the past.

In other words it is neither intuitively plausible nor, in all probability, factually correct that the relative share of income going to labor has remained constant enough in the past for this to have provided an adequate guide to wage level movements.

10. Martin Bronfenbrenner, "A Note on Relative Shares and the Elasticity of Factor Substitution," *Journal of Political Economy*, June, 1960, pp. 284-87.

11. Joan Robinson, "The Production Function," *Economic Journal*, March, 1955, pp. 67-72, provides some support for this point.

Further, there is no reason to assume that such constancy as has existed in the past would continue to hold exactly for the future, nor can it be assumed that secular constancy means, or should mean, short period constancy as well.

But, under propositions three and four it is not necessary to assume approximately constant relative shares without controls for the policy maker to favor maintaining factor shares. It might be that (3) relative shares are non-economically and rather arbitrarily determined in that a change in them would not distort patterns of resource allocation unduly, or (4) maintaining constant relative shares would induce the technological changes needed.

Proposition three is only partially acceptable as an empirical generalization. Some wages and some aspects of the wage bill are importantly influenced by non-economic factors, sometimes by historical accident alone. Accident seems to play a significant role, for example, in determination of the level of the government budget. Nonetheless, existing patterns of resource allocation also are tied closely to consumer preferences and relative costs of production. In this sense present distribution of national income is not a matter of chance or of accident.

Proposition four is even less valid than proposition three. There is an element of truth to the old cliché that necessity is the mother of invention. If there is a relative scarcity of labor (capital) at the existing wage level, and if there are legal obstacles to changing the wage level to correct this situation, employers undoubtedly will learn to economize on whatever resource is scarce. But while entrepreneurial inventiveness can mitigate some of the economic consequences of an inappropriate wage level, the most effective way to foster a proper pattern of resource allocation is to price resources according to relative scarcity. In other words, attempts through wage policy to perpetuate a distribution of income, different from that which would result without controls, can be expected to cause a decline in output.

Propositions three and four are unacceptable generalizations about wage behavior in a market directed economy. They are antithetical to some fundamental beliefs about economic behavior. The propositions are relevant only as indicators of the tolerance the economy has for errors in wage level regulation. Either proposition one or two, however, might be an acceptable generalization. Both conform well enough in principle to marginal productivity theory, designated the macro-economic optimum. Whether or not either of these propositions is factually correct is another matter.

A first problem is to discover what has been the experience of the economy. As noted, empirical data are not at all clear on this point. The significant issues seem to be two in number. Is the apparent constancy of relative income shares an error in measurement, which might imply that the market economy can be typified by gradual change in relative shares? Does the policy maker have any reasonable assurance that past trends would be continued into the future?

A second problem is one of quite a different sort. The wage inflation thesis, accepted here for purposes of analysis, assumes a tendency in the past for wages to move upward too quickly. These increases, it is hypothesized, have price-level implications. If the wage inflation hypothesis is correct, past studies of market behavior are only partially valid as a test of the theoretical value of relative shares, or of any other guide to wage level regulation. Truly significant, of course, is how relative shares should behave. In this connection, not only are past studies of relative share data partially irrelevant to the question of how relative shares ought to shift over time, but they do not give the policy maker correct information about an appropriate starting place.

A satisfactory criterion upon which to base wage level adjustments must do two things. It must indicate the wage level compatible with a given level of prices. It must show how to deal with changing conditions over time. If relative shares are to be the regulatory criterion, the first problem will have to be dealt with in some other way, perhaps through application of the supply and demand principle initially. Beyond this problem, it is evident that the theoretical accuracy of the constant relative shares hypothesis is uncertain. In this it is similar to other wage level criteria, and it offers complications similar to those found in the unregulated market—lack of perfection.

As a final difficulty with the relative shares guide, there are empirical problems. Calculation of changes in the relative share of income going to labor requires consideration and measurement of many factors. The reliability of the calculation hinges upon the accuracy of national incomes data in total and by industry, the availability of an accurate price index to deflate raw data, the ability to define industry boundaries precisely for appraisal of shifts in employment, and wisdom in the application of defini-tional parameters. Calculation of shifts in relative shares is neither simple nor infallible, a fact which has considerable bearing upon the desirability of its use as a wage level guide.

Adjustment According to Productivity Change. Changing out-put per worker provides a third possible criterion for planned ad-justments in the wage level. This concept, popularly referred to as productivity change, is the guide most select. Certainly if volume of literature published is an indication, a great many economists support the view that productivity, in the sense of being equivalent to output per worker, is a useful concept.[12]

Under the "productivity" approach, recommended changes in the wage bill would be based upon anticipated changes in output per worker. For example, an anticipated "productivity" increase of three per cent per year would provide the basis for a recom-mended average increase of three per cent per year in the wage level.

In practice, a wage level guide of this kind would enjoy many similarities with regulation according to relative share data. Past stability of the relationship between percentage increases in the real wage and output per worker increases has paralleled closely

12. For a partial bibliography of pre-1957 productivity writings see U. S. Bureau of Labor Statistics, *Productivity: A Bibliography*, Department of Labor Bulletin No. 1226 (Washington: U. S. Government Printing Office, 1957). Repre-sentative of some of the post-1957 writings are: Arthur Smithies, "Produc-tivity, Real Wages, and Economic Growth. *Quarterly Journal of Economics*, May 1960, pp. 189-205; John W. Kendrick, *Productivity Trends in the United States* (Princeton: National Bureau of Economic Research, 1961); George Stigler, "Economic Problems in Measuring Changes in Productivity," *Output, Input, and Productivity Measurement, Studies in Income and Wealth*, Vol. XXV (Princeton: National Bureau of Economic Research, 1961); John W. Kendrick and Ryuzo Sato, "Factor Prices, Productivity, and Economic Growth," *American Economic Review*, December, 1963, pp. 974-1003; Evsey Domar, "Total Productivity and the Quality of Capital," *Journal of Political Economy*, December, 1963, pp. 586-88; Evsey D. Domar, *et al.*, "Economic Growth and Productivity in the United States, Canada, United Kingdom, Germany and Japan in the Post-War Period," *The Review of Economics and Statistics,* February, 1964, pp. 33-40; Thomas A. Wilson and Otto Eckstein, "Short-Run Productivity Behavior in U. S. Manufacturing," *The Review of Economics and Statistics*, February, 1964, pp. 41-54; D. Dacy, "Price and Productivity Index for a Nonhomogenous Prod-uct," *Journal of the American Statistical Association,* June, 1964, pp. 469-80; Zvi Griliches and Dale W. Jorgenson, "Sources of Measured Productivity Change: Capital Input," *American Economic Review*, May 1965, pp. 50-61; and Fredric Q. Raines, "Price and Productivity Trends in Manufacturing Industries," *The Review of Economics and Statistics*, August, 1967, pp. 393-403.

the stability of labor's relative income share. Indeed the former often is recommended as a means of accomplishing the latter.[13] Hence, perhaps the most significant distinction between the two guides of output per worker and relative share data is an administrative one. Output per worker concentrates upon the level of wages directly rather than upon the total of wages paid. For this reason calculations of output per worker are somewhat simpler to make, although they still may be quite complex.

In general, while the guides of relative shares and output per worker are not precisely identical in their result, because when factor proportions change application of the "productivity" (output per worker) guide could involve a change in labor's relative income share, the arguments against attempted stabilization of labor's relative income share also can be applied against relating general wage changes to output per worker changes. Past correlation does not demonstrate future correlation. The relationship in the past has not been perfect, and this is especially significant in view of the large absolute change needed before the percentage change becomes measurable. Past experience, given the wage inflation hypothesis, is an incomplete guide to future wage policy action.

As a final problem associated with implementation of "productivity" as a guide to wage level adjustment, output per worker can be variously defined.[14] The definition selected would affect the magnitude of recommended changes in the wage bill. However, which definition of output per worker would yield a wage bill closest to the marginal productivity optimum would be more a matter of chance than of logic. The correct average wage level adjustment would depend upon the supply of labor relative to the demand for it, not upon output per worker.

Adjustment in Response to Political or Social Pressures. A fourth method of determining the wage bill would be to suggest

13. See, for example, William Fellner, *Competition Among the Few* (New York: Alfred Knopf, 1949), pp. 311-21. In part Fellner apparently argues in favor of this technique because it is one that helps overcome such problems as how to handle a change in the percentage of workers that are self employed. William Fellner, *Trends and Cycles in Economic Activity*, pp. 260-65.

14. The number of formulae that might be used are legion. For a brief survey of a great number of possibilities see T. E. Easterfield, *Productivity Measurement in Great Britain* (London: Department of Scientific and Industrial Research, 1959).

that the wage authority ignore pressures for a general wage increase or for an increase in particular markets, if they could be resisted without serious social and/or political repercussions. There would be no direct criterion for determination of the wage bill other than the general injunction that wage increases should be avoided whenever and wherever feasible.

A policy designed to minimize incremental increases in wages in this way would be approximately equivalent to policies of most countries during war periods. Some countries currently under wage control programs also seem to accept this sort of regulatory criterion to a large degree. Presumably the argument in favor of such a guide would be: The significant problem is to restrain excessive wage increases. Restraining increases would not result in a too inappropriate wage level. And allocative problems would not be overly severe because of concurrent development of social and/or political pressures for corrective action. The success of such a program would depend upon a number of factors. The intensity of pressures on the wage level is one factor. The resolution with which the regulatory authority withstood these pressures is another. Also important is the degree of compatibility with wage pattern criteria developed.

Intensity of pressures on the wage level might be slight, as in the case where most inflation is demand-pull in type and adequately controlled by general stabilization policy. Or inflationary pressures might be relatively strong, as with acute cost-push inflation pressures. Intensity of pressures on the wage level also is a function of institutional practices. A nation which experiences general strikes, for example, probably can be expected to find pressures on the wage level stronger than they otherwise would be.

Similarly, the resolution with which the wage authority resists upward wage pressures would vary depending upon the particular situation and upon the institutional environment. During wartime or other national emergency a wage authority may find it possible to be quite resolute because of popular support for actions taken in the "national interest." Relatively open economies and/or economies with a continuing balance of payments problem, which have a greater awareness of the need for inflation control, exemplify another situation where inflationary pressures might be resisted more successfully.

The institutional setting also is an important determinant of the degree of resoluteness which may be mustered. For example, the administrative organization of the wages authority and the powers of investigation and enforcement granted to it have a significant bearing on the stand of the regulatory authority faced with pressures on the wage level.

But, whether or not circumstances are favorable for the wages authority, it is unreasonable to expect a wage bill influenced by political or social pressures to approximate one dictated by marginal productivity theory or to be as economically satisfactory as a wage level otherwise determined. A system so informal and lacking in objective criteria as that described gives little assurance of yielding satisfactory results.

As a final problem the suggestion that wage increases be resisted whenever and wherever possible contains implications for wage pattern adjustment. Such a macro formula would be incompatible with the formula for wage pattern adjustment suggested later in this book, and it would interfere with any formula for adjustment of relative wage rates that rationally might be suggested. This, by itself, is perhaps sufficiently serious a criticism to eliminate adjustment according to political and/or social pressures as a possible guide. It is sufficiently serious not because a wage bill so obtained must, of necessity, be unacceptable, but because other criteria exist that promise greater likelihood of success.

The Criterion Appropriate. None of the four guides to wage level determination discussed appears measurably superior to the others, although adjustment in response to political and/or social pressures appears slightly less workable than any of the other guides.

Changes in output per worker has the attractive attribute of relative simplicity of calculation. It also could be a comparatively precise and readily understandable tool. However, the case for its theoretical appropriateness is not so strong.

Adjustment according to relative shares involves intense problems of definition and measurement, although even so these may not be so acute as for the supply and demand criterion. Adjustment so as to maintain constancy of income shares has the advantage of directly controlling the wage bill rather than the wage level, but it shares, with the output per worker guide, the disadvantage of a weak theoretical case favoring its use.

Adjustment according to supply and demand, while suggesting

more intense problems of calculation than adjustment according to either output per worker or relative incomes shares, also holds forth promise of yielding a somewhat more appropriate guide to wage level changes. Supply and demand are difficult to measure, and measurement involves a number of definitional issues which are at least as complex and probably more so than those connected with measurement of relative income shares. The redeeming feature of the supply and demand approach is that, next to direct application of marginal productivity theory, it comes closest to being the logically correct criterion to apply.

EVALUATION OF THE CRITERIA

Calculation of the wage bill is exceedingly complicated and has many pitfalls. Given some sort of national incomes policy, there are various possible combinations of levels of output, employment, wage rates, government spending, and taxation compatible with a given price-level. Because of the definitional and empirical limitations facing the policy maker, the "equilibrium set" selected inevitably will involve considerable arbitrary decision making. There is no doubt that such a process of wage determination will yield levels of output, growth, income distribution, and therefore welfare different from and inferior to that which would be obtained in a theoretical utopia. But it would be improper to move from this to a position in which it is asserted that a regulated market is less perfect than an unregulated market because the wage bill, in part, might be determined arbitrarily.

In the real world, individual market decisions typically are made in a very halting and uncertain manner. Hence it is that the aggregate wage bill already is determined rather haphazardly. Moreover, there is no valid reason for supposing that over a period of time the market determined wage is randomly dispersed about the economically most desirable level. Wage-push theorists argue that it is not, and this, of course, is the reason why national incomes policy might be considered an appropriate anti-inflation remedy.

According to many who support the wage-push explanation, the phenomenon of a too high wage rate moving upward too quickly means that in order to hold the competitive pace, people individually are forced by economic conditions to follow a wage determination behavior pattern that they do not like in total, would vote against if they had the chance, and would be pleased to have the state regulate away.

All this has implications for the initial efficacy of a macro wage guide, and it provides a point of departure for definitional beginnings. It is less helpful in providing a guide to longer term wage level policies and in evaluating the effectiveness of whatever policies are developed.

National incomes policy used to influence the national wage level, to be an immediate improvement over the unregulated market, need only decide if the economy is in a period of relative prosperity. If so, upward wage pressures are present by definition, and the sole remaining initial questions of policy would be: how thoroughly to restrain upward wage pressures, and how to coordinate other economic policies. As an additional advantage, policy decisions could be judged, initially, through comparison of levels of output and employment after a national incomes policy program had been established with levels of output and employment before controls. If the economy generally experienced over a period of time a higher level of employment and output than had been the rule previously, this would be encouraging. If not, seemingly, an administrative change would be indicated. Moreover, such an evaluation procedure, while logically suggesting the supply and demand approach of course, also would be compatible with the other three guides to wage adjustment discussed in this chapter.

However, as time passed and the economy changed, pre-national incomes policy experiences obviously would be less and less relevant as a test of effectiveness. In addition, over a period of time errors inherent in wage level calculation methods as well as problems associated with uneven compliance throughout the economy with wage level changes recommended would be likely to lead to a cumulative wage level error. The unregulated market, were it to experience an increasingly inappropriate wage level, would experience a build-up of forces working to return real wages to a level more compatible with the economic environment. This would be much less likely to occur under a system of guided wages such as those outlined.

If wage-push inflation is a continuing problem for our economy, national incomes policy might yield a general level of wages more nearly compatible with price stabilizing monetary and fiscal policy than past wage levels. But this would become less likely as time progressed. However, ability to choose a level of wages more compatible with price-level stability than market determined wages obviously is not an inclusive test of the overall effectiveness of a national incomes policy program. Macro-economic wage level changes are accomplished only by adjustment of individual wage rates in individual markets so that the total of wages is what it should be. To be effective, a wage control system must influence relative wages in an appropriate fashion. Whether or not useful guides upon which to base such adjustments exist is the subject of the following chapter. Whether or not practical administrative problems can be overcome so that the guides might be followed is the subject of Chapters 9 and 10. Moreover, judgements about the probable success of achieving and maintaining desirable movements in the national, or macro-economic wage, are predicated upon the assumption that no attempt is made cyclically to adjust the level of wages, as governmental influencing of the wage level is bound to be much too awkward and uncertain for this. Efforts at frequent adjustment of the level of wages almost certainly would engender conflicts with stabilization policy. It seems unlikely that even approximately workable criteria for short period adjustment of the wage level could be found.

By way of illustration of this last point, recent U.S. wage guidepost policy pronouncements have suggested that anywhere from a 3.0 to 3.5 per cent annual productivity improvement factor might be appropriate. However, it seems likely that uncertainty concerning the proper "productivity" calculation is mainly a consequence of cyclical rather than secular changes in output per worker figures. The analysis at this point in the chapter cautions strongly against cyclical variation in wage adjustment formulas because of attendant monetary and fiscal stabilization policy problems. This caution against cyclical variation in wage adjustment formulas particularly is to be noted for those situations where guidepost type policies are widely adhered to—a situation for which the United States presently is a poor parallel, obviously.

Chapter 8

WAGE PATTERN CRITERIA

THE LEVEL OF WAGES affects the pattern of wages appropriate. The pattern of wages affects the level of wages appropriate. It is clear that the solution to micro- and macro-economic aspects of the wage[1] setting problem must be either simultaneous or nearly so. This means that if wages are to be influenced by a central administrative authority, the criteria applied will need to involve the technique of successive approximation in planning and execution. Application of simultaneous equations would be impractical. At first blush this in itself seems a vitiating criticism of detailed government involvement in the wage setting process. Fortunately, as indicated earlier although the wage determination process is highly complicated, things are not quite this bad.

First, in the absence of governmentally established limits to private bargaining over wages, wage decisions would be made by the market, and market allocation of resources is very imperfect. This substantially reduces the test of performance that would be required of any criteria established by the government. It is not necessary that the pattern of resources developed be ideal or nearly ideal. Instead, resource allocation after government involvement must be as good as, or nearly as good as, that presently existing. Particularly since the postulate for the moment is that, in the

1. Again the reader is reminded that the definition of a wage is a complex task as any definition must include consideration of fringe benefits and basis of wage payment. These problems are discussed in Chapter 10.

absence of regulation, there would be a tendency for the wage level to be much too high, this is a much more realistic objective. The possibility now exists that wage level adjustment by administrative fiat might represent a substantial improvement over the unregulated market and that, on balance, government influence of wage adjustment might be favored in spite of certain allocative problems. Whether these allocative problems will occur, and the severity of them, is a subject yet to be discussed.

Second, the economy is sufficiently stable and consistent that reasonably accurate economic predictions often are possible. Many basic decisions about wage patterns and wage levels need not be revised every period. Criteria developed might survey and act upon predictable trends. Continued urban expansion, greater numbers of white collar workers, substantial migration of unskilled workers from Southern states, increasing emphasis on service industries, and a rising percentage of high school and college graduates exemplify trends that have strong implications for wage policy, both micro-economic and macro-economic.

Finally, a national wages policy would not have to be formulated in the context of an economic vacuum, but could work with a going concern, an economy already in existence. For this reason necessary wage level and wage pattern changes would be less extreme than if it were necessary to move to an entirely new situation. Of course, as previously pointed out, many policy choices would get cumulatively more difficult as time progressed. Market behavior prior to institution of a national incomes policy would become less and less relevant as a guide to policy action.

Assume now that a case for some sort of national incomes policy exists. A next question is: what must be some general characteristics of a wage administration program? To a large degree the answer to this would depend upon the specific administrative procedures used in influencing the wage setting process. But, at the outset note may be taken of four overriding principles that pertain to adjustments recommended in particular market situations.

First, the wage adjustment process must be flexible. In this respect the program for influencing individual wage rates in individual markets must differ measurably from that employed in this country and many others during World War II. True, World War II experiences showed that changes in wage patterns and in wage levels were inevitable.[2] But these changes were kept to a minimum.

Under present assumptions this would not be possible. With a longer range control program, one that was expected to become a permanent part of economic life, provision for change in relative wage rates would have to be a key feature of the administration process. Ours is a dynamic society. Patterns of consumption and of production are continually shifting. They are shifting in response to changes in businesses' cost structures, to changes in workers' tastes and preferences for work, and to changes in consumers' tastes and preferences for goods. Compensation through the price mechanism for these changes is essential to induce a satisfactory pattern of output and employment.[3]

A second overriding principle which must be kept in mind is that there is a tolerance limit to administrative expenses for a national incomes policy. If administrative expenses were not a problem, possibly a program might be devised which would yield a highly satisfactory pattern of wage rates. But the hypothesis is doubtful, administrative budgets are not unlimited, and in any event the present study is not designed to examine the case for so extreme a program, one that ultimately would involve quite thoroughgoing control of all factors of production.

All this suggests that, whatever the micro-economic adjustment procedure selected through which both micro and macro policy will be implemented, it cannot be all-pervasive. Existing or anticipated socio-economic institutions must be capitalized upon to complement efforts of the responsible government authority. In a sense this is no more than should be expected of any good system of control. A good many years ago J. M. Clark suggested:[4]

2. As earlier noted, under regulation wage level changes should be occasional or follow a stable and predictable pattern over time so as to facilitate monetary and fiscal policy and wage pattern regulation.

3. One of the disturbing features of the current U. S. wage guideposts is that, in application, no provision for this sort of change is being made. The guideposts, as formally stated, acknowledge the need for relative wage rate adjustment, but in application to particular markets this fact is being ignored. Abba Lerner is a particular critic of this approach. See, for example, his 1966 Richard T. Ely lecture to the American Economic Association, "Employment Theory and Employment Policy," *American Economic Review*, May, 1967, pp. 1-18. In other words, current reliance upon "unofficial" departures from the guideposts to effect needed allocational changes is too inexact a procedure upon which to place serious reliance.

4. *Social Control of Business* (Chicago: University of Chicago Press, 1926), p. 17.

A good system of control must meet a number of tests, some of them quite difficult. (1) It must be democratic. . . . (2) It should know what it wants. . . . (3) It must be powerful. . . . (4) It must be efficient, and at the same time it must not destroy the efficiency of the thing it is regulating. (5) It must economize coercion. (6) It must utilize all the strongest and most persistent motives of human nature, both generous and selfish; hope of reward, fear of punishment, and those loyalties, persuasions, and suggestions which have nothing to do with rewards and punishments, but which rest upon the deeper fact that the individual is essentially a part of the community. (7) The duties imposed must be simple enough to be understood. . . . (8) Control must be guided by experience or be wisely experimental. (9) It must be adaptable. (10) It must be far reaching. . . . (11) And lastly, social control must be capable of progressively raising the level of mankind.

But in another sense the Clarkian guides are quite different from what is needed. Clark, and those who have enumerated guides similar to his, had in mind requisites for a good system of control. The problem here is a more special case. Unless the system of control is a good one the preference should be for no control at all.

A third overriding principle for government influence of wage pattern adjustment is that, as with guides to wage level determination, theoretical perfection is not necessarily the most appropriate attribute for a good control program. While it may be reasonably clear, on the theoretical level, what factors determine the wage rate appropriate in a given instance, this theory may have little or no relevance as a practical guide to policy action. Factors which are believed to be important considerations for the businessman may be particularly difficult to isolate and measure. For this reason, it may be necessary to suggest a theoretically inferior, but administratively superior, adjustment index.

A fourth and final overriding principle is that the selected guide to wage rate adjustment must be quantifiable. A wage policy which allows adjustment in individual wages to be primarily dependent upon subjective evaluations is inadequate. The principles upon which judgments are to be made must be explicit both in number and in relative importance, and they must be measurable.

A THEORETICAL FOUNDATION

Some theoretical foundation is an essential prerequisite to evaluation of criteria for wage rate adjustment. But selection of a standard by which to judge relative wage rates involves a number of questions of economic welfare which are not easily solved.

This work will assume that an optimum pattern of resource allocation is served if wages in individual markets are set at the point where marginal revenue product equals the average cost of labor acquisition, *i.e.*, supply under competition. There is some theoretical basis for this assumption, but it is by no means perfect. An important postulate of traditional economic theory is that, given perfectly competitive markets, an optimum pattern of resource allocation can occur only when workers receive the value of their marginal product. However, where imperfect markets exist the analysis must be amended. At this point difficulties are encountered.

As suggested, one possibility would be to apply what might be called the marginal productivity concept and set the wage where the marginal revenue product schedule and the average cost of labor acquisition schedule intersect. But this is only one possibility out of several. In essence the suggestion is that output be set where marginal cost equals marginal revenue. But welfare theorists are in general agreement that, while the issues involved are quite complex, a better pattern of resource allocation might occur if output universally were set where price equals marginal cost. For the labor market, in other words, the suggestion would be for wages and employment to be set where average cost of labor acquisition equals value of the marginal product.[5]

This alternative is discarded. It represents so substantial a departure from the pricing behavior of unregulated markets that wage controls so directed could not simply be an overlay imposed upon the existing economy. To implement such a proposal it would be necessary, instead, to completely reorder the economic system. Perhaps the idea has merit; but consideration of it is a subject unto itself, is not the purpose of the present work, and clearly has not been in the minds of those who have suggested wage controls as a possible means of dealing with wage inflation.

On the other hand, the suggestion that wages be set where the

5. See, for example, William J. Baumol, *Economic Theory and Operations Analysis* (Englewood Cliffs: Prentice-Hall, Inc., 1961), pp. 246-75.

marginal revenue product schedule and average cost of labor acquisition schedule intersect, in each labor market, also is open to a number of substantive criticisms. Such a pricing procedure suggests application of criteria which the market now neglects because of problems of measurement. Such a pricing procedure precludes the possibility of using wage policy to offset a market imperfection outside of the labor market, in order to encourage a more perfect pattern of resource allocation.[6] Such a pricing policy raises a question of equity where marginal revenue product is rising instead of falling or where the production function is not linear and homogenous, as in cases where paying each factor its marginal revenue product would more than or less than exhaust the total product. As an additional impact, in imperfectly competitive labor markets, application of such a pricing policy would result in a relative wage rate and level of employment different from that which would have occurred in the absence of government controls over wage bargaining.

Under the special case of bilateral monopoly, it usually is argued that, in the unregulated market, the level of employment would tend to be determined where the marginal revenue product and average cost of labor acquisition schedules intersected,[7] although this would not have to be the case. But it is contended that the wage set would depend upon relative bargaining power. If this analysis is correct, application of the marginal revenue productivity concept previously selected as the "optimum" goal almost certainly would mean a change in the relative wage from that which would occur in the absence of regulation. It might mean a change in the level of employment as well.

Similarly, application of the adopted marginal revenue productivity concept would result in a change in the wage paid, and in the level of employment, in any imperfect market. To the degree that a given rate of wages is administratively established, the illusion is present that the labor supply and the demand for labor,

6. Definition of a perfect pattern of resource allocation is a subject of some controversy, the roots of which lie in differing ethical judgments. But this definitional disagreement is peripheral to the main issue, which is that strict application of the above-described marginal productivity concept will not meet completely any of the usual descriptions of perfection and that, in certain situations, another regulatory formula might do better.

7. Bernard F. Haley, "Value and Distribution," *A Survey of Contemporary Economics*, Volume I, Howard S. Ellis, ed. (Homewood: Richard D. Irwin, Inc., 1948), pp. 23-24.

facing the individual firm or the individual, are perfectly elastic up to the point of most profitable operation. Thus, on assumption of downsloping labor demand and upsloping labor supply schedules, once the government sets the wage, manufacturers no longer would have an economic incentive to pay labor less than its marginal value product. Equally, labor would have no reason to attempt to force a wage rate above the average cost of acquisition of labor.

The difficulty with the marginal revenue productivity concept as a practical guide to wage rate regulation is that it is not possible to collect the data necessary for its implementation. To do so with any degree of accuracy would require that wage administrators have access to all those business records which bear on product demand, labor supply, and labor's marginal physical productivity. Many of these variables cannot be delineated from existing financial records. Therefore, wage administrators also would have to be privy to the considered business judgment of businessmen involved.

Even apart from matters of enforcement these are unreasonable standards. The idea of direct application of this theory must be discarded, even though marginal revenue productivity will remain the assumed theoretical optimum. It will be used to judge the wage determination criteria to be discussed, output per worker, ability to pay, comparative wages, and minimum budgets, any one or all of which might be suggested, incorrectly, as guides for relative wage rate adjustment. It also will be used to judge the criterion selected as most acceptable to guide micro-economic wage adjustments, Abba Lerner's surplus-shortage criterion, or something quite similar to it in principle of operation.

UNACCEPTABLE GUIDES TO MICRO-ECONOMIC WAGE DETERMINATION

When suggesting a means for determining the economically appropriate wage pattern, it is necessary to understand that a number of criteria which have been used in the past by private industry, by trade unions, and by the government would not be acceptable. The task at this point, then, is to investigate what might be called "bogus" criteria for relative wage rate adjustment. This investigation should accomplish two purposes. It should demonstrate why certain criteria, which in the past have enjoyed considerable popularity as guides to wage rate adjustment and wage rate evaluation would not be acceptable in the present context. It should yield insights into difficulties and problems to be faced when attempting to set the micro-economic wage.

The criteria to be discussed in this section are grouped under four headings: output per worker, ability to pay, comparative wages, and minimum budgets. It cannot be stressed too thoroughly, however, that these criteria never have been employed in the context which this work envisages and discussion of them is not intended to imply that they have been or ought to be suggested for such use. Further, while the criteria are discussed separately, with the possible exception of output per worker, it is doubtful that any one of them ever has been used as the sole determinant of wages. During World War I, for example, the U.S. government relied not upon one, but upon two criteria in its wage setting procedures, comparative wages and minimum budgets.[8] During World War II primary emphasis was on comparative wages, but productivity (in the output per worker sense), ability to pay, and minimum budgets also were considered on some occasions.[9]

The criteria to be discussed in this section are also somewhat indeterminate. The terms used, in their simple and elemental form, are not adequately defined. They are subject to mutation over time. Indeed in some cases they appear to escape careful definition

8. In adjudication of labor disputes the War Labor Conference Board put forth three criteria which were accepted when the National War Labor Board was created by Presidential proclamation on April 8, 1918. These criteria were (1) ". . . in fixing wages, hours and conditions of labor regard should always be had to the labor standards, wage scales, and other conditions, prevailing in the localities affected." (2) "The right of all workers, including common laborers, to a living wage is hereby declared." (3) "In fixing wages, minimum rates of pay shall be established which will insure the subsistence of the worker and his family in health and reasonable comfort." U. S. Bureau of Labor Statistics, *National War Labor Board*, Bulletin No. 287 (Washington: U. S. Government Printing Office, 1922), pp. 33-34.

9. General policies of wage rate adjustment fluctuated a good deal during the war period. A brief summary of criteria used for the greater part of the war is to be found in Executive Order of the President No. 9250 which said in part: "The National War Labor Board shall not approve any increase in the wage rates prevailing on September 15, 1942, unless such increase is necessary to correct maladjustments or inequalities, to eliminate substandards of living, to correct gross inequities, or to aid in the effective prosecution of the war." Greater detail concerning wages administration policy during World War II is to be found in *The Termination Report of the War Labor Board*, Vol. 1 (Washington: U.S. Government Printing Office, 1946), pp. 178-289.

altogether. To illustrate this, what exactly was meant by the World War II dictum that wages should be adjusted in such a way as to preserve traditional differentials while removing existing inequities?[10] This is awfully nebulous. Such a definition is subject to different interpretations from one economic group to another, from one culture to another, from one time to another, etc. It also is subject to different interpretations within the above named groups. Moreover, when an attempt is made to compress all of wage theory into a phrase of this sort, a certain aura of the slogan cannot be avoided. It is then quite likely that the concept or slogan will represent more of a rallying cry than a concrete idea. Definition of the words "traditional" and "inequity" often ebb and flow with the gains and reversals of the particular bargaining experience in which context they are used.

Thus, there are obvious faults inherent in the use of criteria of the sort just alluded to. Still, it would be far too easy and not at all accurate to conclude that the terms are devoid of economic meaning and that study of them cannot be instructive. They are criteria that have been used in the past both by government and by industry. Most assuredly they are criteria that will continue to be employed in the future. In these situations they seem to work or are capable of being made workable. While in many cases they are no doubt just a cover for the true criteria used, they also seem to embody economic content of their own. In short, such criteria cannot be used for national incomes policy purposes but that does not mean they are without value or that study of them cannot be instructive.

Output Per Worker. In contexts other than that of national incomes policy as an inflation deterrent, it is frequently suggested that changes in output per worker, more often referred to as productivity changes, provide an appropriate guide to wage adjustment. But as a guide to relative wage rate adjustment, and in the context of an incomes policy to combat wage inflation, a measure of this sort clearly is unworkable. In general the wages of labor are, and should be, dependent upon its productivity. But this does not mean output per worker, and the statement can be correct in the case of the individual firm only when labor supply is perfectly inelastic.

10. General Order 1-A of the National War Labor Board, November 6, 1942.

As noted in Chapter 7, some writers contend that average percentage changes in output per worker for the entire nation would provide an adequate guide to adjustment of the general level of wages. This point of view might be correct. It would depend upon the definition of productivity selected. It would depend upon the nature of the short-run supply of labor and capital in aggregate. It also would depend upon the way in which these schedules shift over time. It is evident, however, that the generalization that wages should be dependent upon output per worker cannot be extended to a series of dissimilar markets.

Within the economy, factor supply elasticities differ from situation to situation. Demand elasticities also are subject to variation. So too, rates of growth over time differ greatly among geographical areas, among industries, and among firms. This suggests that factor supply and demand elasticities in different markets change in different ways. Incremental increases or decreases in relative wage rates, therefore, need to vary from place to place, from industry to industry, from firm to firm, from worker occupation to worker occupation, and over a period of time.

To give just one illustration: assume an identical shift in the productivity of labor in two labor market situations, one where the supply of labor is perfectly elastic, the other where the supply of labor is perfectly inelastic. In the first case, traditional economic theory predicts a wage change in the amount of the change in labor productivity, but no change in employment. In the second case, traditional theory predicts no change in the wage, but a change in employment. According to this same theory, labor supply curves of intermediate slope would be accompanied by an intermediate result, *i.e.*, some change in the wage rate and some change in employment. The ratio of the result, of course, would depend upon the relative elasticity of labor supply and demand.

In other words, in terms of the earlier discussed marginal productivity theory, the wage appropriate in a given instance would depend upon: (1) The nature of the marginal revenue product curve, rather than the average physical product curve, for the labor factor in question. (2) The nature of the supply curve for the labor desired. Considerable variation from one economic situation to another can be expected in these two categories. It thus would be pure coincidence if the wage change appropriate in a given instance should exactly equal the percentage change in output per worker in that market.[11] Conceivably, wages and percentage changes in physical output per worker need not even be positively correlated.

Ability to Pay. A second criterion for wage rate determination is some form of the ability to pay concept. It is doubtful if there is, today, any bargaining session that takes place in which ability to pay is not a factor. Often it is explicitly referred to. Not only is the concept of ability to pay typically a part of the actual bargaining session, but frequently it occupies a prominent role in the general publicity releases of labor, management, and/or other interested parties to a particular bargaining session as well. Moreover, there often is considerable dispute as to whether or not, in a given instance, ability to pay actually does exist, for measurement of the concept is an extremely difficult task.

In one sense of the term, determinants of ability to pay are as explained by marginal revenue productivity theory. But if this is to be the accepted definition nothing more need be said. The reader is referred to the previous section dealing with that subject. However, many times it is suggested that relative differences in profits, somehow defined, are an appropriate index of relative ability to pay.

The proposition that relatively higher (lower) profits are an indication of inappropriately low (high) wage rates seemingly would involve the presumption that profits are or ought to be exclusively a derivative of wages. This is clearly false. Relative profits are only partly a function of relative wage rates, and then, under conditions of perfectly functioning economic markets, just in the short-run. Short-run profits also are a function of other factor costs, product demand, rates of interest, risk, and uncertainty, plus degree of monopoly power. This explains why the extent to which wages have been a function of ability to pay in the past has varied over the business cycle, and with the industry, the firm, the geographical location, and sometimes with the labor market in question.

There is much to recommend use of ability to pay as a wage determination criterion by labor and by management, as changes

11. The reader is reminded that the definition of appropriate, established earlier, is where the marginal revenue product and average cost of labor acquisition schedules intersect and that in imperfectly competitive labor markets this "optimum" is not the same as the market equilibrium.

in profits are one signal of changes in labor's marginal revenue product. But ability to pay is not a measure that is adaptable to the requirements of an administrative authority charged with responsibility for attempting to influence or set wages throughout the economy on a reasonably clear, consistent, and economically "fair" basis. Definition of ability to pay, insofar as it is used as a determinant of wages, seems to depend upon the particular context of application. This is because, as indicated, ability to pay is a partial rather than a complete determinant of wage changes. Hence, the concept is unreliable as a general policy tool. It is an elusive idea that seems to escape careful and precise definition. Or if it is precisely defined it is not generally applicable.

Comparative Wages. Wage comparisons are another category of wage determination criteria that have been resorted to frequently. There are, of course, many possible types of wage comparisons, but they all have in common comparison with some "key" relationships (s). Comparisons of some sort are at least implied in the concepts of "preserving traditional differentials while removing existing inequities," "equal pay for equal work," wages based upon "precedent," and "skill" differentials, to name some prominent examples.

Individually, these are capable of definition. But, as with the ability to pay example, their definition is exceptionally difficult and subject to change from place to place and from time to time. Naturally, if demand and supply relationships affecting labor were to remain unchanged, if no new trades were developed, if labor retained its present skill and abilities, etc., the problem of wage comparisons would not be particularly difficult. But these are the conditions of stability of relative wage rates and of no need for change. If forces pushing for a change in the wage structure are introduced, the rise of a new skill or trade or a change in the demand-supply relationships within a given trade, then a comparative criterion well may prove inadequate to the task for which it was designed.

This is not to say that wages determined on a comparative or tradition basis always are inappropriate. Differentials of risk, skill, job prestige,[12] etc., to a large degree determine, and should de-

12. The correlation here is, of course, reverse. The higher the prestige the lower the wage that might be expected. Perhaps college teaching is an example.

termine, wage patterns. The problem is how to interrelate and quantify these factors. The comparative concept is predicated upon the assumption that there are "key" relationships or differentials, which are not determined on a comparative basis, which can be used to guide policy action. It is by analogy to these pre-established "key" relationships that individual wages are determined. This is highly ambiguous. In a changing world, which relationships remain significant, how significant, significant for what?

Minimum Budgets. Some notion of a minimum budget provides another possible standard upon which to base adjustments in relative wage rates. Again this is a concept that has enjoyed frequent use. Concepts with a minimum budget type of connotation used in the past include "a fair day's pay for a fair day's work," "cost of living wage adjustments," a "fair share for labor," and a "living wage."

As a policy guide for adjustment of all wages, the minimum budget idea holds little promise. It cannot be used as the sole criterion for adjustment of relative wage rates if anything like an economic allocation of resources is expected. Its use in any particular area will affect patterns of output and employment. It will result in the overpricing of some labor as evidenced by an unnecessarily high amount of involuntary unemployment. It will result in the underpricing of some labor as evidenced by an unnecessarily high amount of voluntary unemployment. On balance its use in the past at least seems to have been heavily weighted in favor of raising wages of low wage groups, but not necessarily lowering wages of high wage groups. Hence the possibility exists that introduction of this guide to any degree will provide macro-economic complications as well as micro-economic complications, a point which will be discussed at slightly greater length in Chapter 10.

It may be argued on welfare grounds that a wage above the market equilibrium sometimes is desirable. Possible arguments include: (1) a belief that lack of occupational or regional employment opportunities induce labor mobility in the "appropriate" direction much more quickly and with less eventual hardship than a wage differential, (2) a belief that workers are better off not working in a particular area than working for a "low" wage, or perhaps (3) a belief that the unemployment and hardship suffered by a few as a result of imposition of a minimum wage in a particular area is more than offset by the gains in welfare enjoyed by those whose services in the area or occupation are retained and whose wages are increased. This latter argument, it might be added is most applicable where the demand for labor is relatively inelastic and where the welfare position of the consumer is ignored.

On the other hand the case for a wage below the market equilibrium, which is the necessary concomitant of wages above market equilibrium, is much less clear. There is, then, serious question as to whether the minimum budget idea ought to be used to guide wage policy at all since increases in some wages unmatched by decreases elsewhere will produce macro-economic problems. Further, since arguments in favor of application of the minimum budget type of concept cannot reasonably be carried to the extreme of saying that it would be best if all workers had an equal wage, the policy maker is left with some very serious questions about how thoroughly the concept ought to be applied, if it should be applied at all.

Summary. Four criteria for relative wage rate determination now have been examined: output per worker, ability to pay, comparative wages, and minimum budgets. All were found highly unsatisfactory for national incomes policy purposes, largely because they are unsatisfactory from an administrative standpoint.

The criteria discussed either have depended upon quantification of factors that are virtually impossible to measure, as marginal revenue product and marginal cost of labor acquisition; or else they have depended upon definition of terms, as ability to pay, which cannot be uniquely defined from place to place, from worker occupation to worker occupation, from firm to firm, or from industry to industry, let alone from time to time.

The criteria suggested thus far are not simple. They are not easy to apply. Frequently they are not adequately flexible. They do not rely at all heavily on the regulated group for aid in data collection, wage computations, or enforcement.

MARKET EMPLOYMENT DATA

As has been shown, quite a number of writers have hinted at and perhaps argued for particular administrative criteria they believed to be satisfactory for determining or influencing appropriate wage patterns by administrative fiat. But, regardless of the way in which these proposals are phrased, quite often they can be reduced to the basic principle that so far as is possible, individual wage rates should be encouraged to conform to relative degrees of labor scarcity (or surplus) existing in each individual area, that is according to market employment data. Objections to earlier discussed proposals heighten the attractiveness of the market employment guide.

In order to implement the market employment or surplus-shortage idea, obviously, it is necessary, first, to develop a system of measurement, by which areas of labor surplus (or shortage) are identified; and second, to devise a formula by which the signal of unbalanced employment can be translated into the remedy of wage adjustment.

As indicated in Chapter 5, a frequently seized upon proposal would tie market employment goals to existing levels of national unemployment. Thus, three per cent unemployment nationally suggests, for purposes of relative wage adjustment, the goal of three per cent unemployed in each individual labor market; two per cent unemployed nationally, suggests a two per cent market by market goal, and so on.

The primary advantage claimed for this sort of approach is that wage adjustments might be made to depend upon the relative eagerness of workers to move into or out of a specific area, industry, or job classification at a given wage rate, combined with the need for them in each category as determined by what employers are willing to pay. It is argued that this means no complex definitions need be formulated. The principles upon which wages might be determined are relatively simple in character and comparatively few in number. Desire to work would be presumed to exist whenever prospective employees actively seek employment in a given area. Desire to employ, which is derived from consumer demand, would be presumed to exist whenever an employer registers job vacancies.

Thus, although the abilities and job preferences of prospective employees will be subject to change over time, as will the needs and preferences of employers, the policy criteria for wage rate adjustment would not have to change. The policy maker could continue to rely upon the market to provide data necessary to the calculation of areas of relative labor surplus and shortage. No other welfare criteria or value judgments need be applied.

In the main, the administrative authority would be using the same sort of wage determination criteria that the "free market" employs. Since this sort of criteria is generally intelligible to laymen, any of several groups, even though operating on an independent basis, presumably should be able to come up with a wage pattern approximately identical to that established by a central regulatory authority. Thus, the originating point for a change in existing wage rates could be any of several, rather diverse sources. Enforcement possibilities, presumably, would be equally varied.

Basically, then, the market employment data approach is for recommended wage adjustments in individual markets to be tied to particular market supply and demand characteristics. But, of course, market demand is to be estimated indirectly by the degree of labor surplus (shortage) existing, rather than directly by means of the marginal productivity approach. The supply and demand objective has obvious merit. The relevant question is, can it be achieved through the market employment data medium. This leads directly to analysis of what sometimes has been termed details of administration, analysis of which is the subject of Chapters 9 and 10.

Obviously it is impossible to establish and implement administrative criteria that will yield an ideal pattern of wage rates. But thus far the analysis of this book merely hints at the possibility of developing and maintaining a "workable" pattern of wage rates by administrative action. Before any sort of a strong case for, or against, a national incomes policy can be said to exist, a closer examination of these "administrative" aspects of the problem is needed. As a practical matter, is it likely that the administrative task suggested by the market employment criterion is an achievable one? What sorts of problems would be encountered in the course of implementing the proposal? How might the problems that arise be dealt with? These will be topics of the next two chapters.

Chapter 9

IMPLEMENTATION OF THE CONTROL PROPOSAL: DATA COLLECTION AND EVALUATION

THERE IS A MYRIAD of difficulties that arise from attempting to superimpose a national incomes policy program of the surplus-shortage type on an economy such as that of the United States. These problems may be classified, generally, as administrative aspects of wages control. Administrative aspects of wages control comprise a subject that is not very thoroughly treated by most of those who advocate some sort of national incomes policy as an anti-inflationary device.

This is unfortunate for, given a national incomes policy program of the sort outlined, intense problems surround the tasks of recognition, classification, and measurement of areas of relative labor surplus (shortage). One cannot suggest a control criterion which demands adjustment of wages according to supply and demand and then relegate such problems as that of measurement to the area of administrative issues. Nor can the problem be avoided by eliminating such matters from the control formula, as in the popular application of the President's "U. S. Wage Guideposts." Either approach would mean that many of the more significant questions of policy and of theory are left unanswered. Control formulae adopted must permit changing wage patterns in accord with changing labor demand and supply conditions prevailing. And administrative procedures by which this can be accomplished are integral to the theory itself. Administration then becomes a crucial issue.

Obviously this work cannot discuss administrative problems extensively. The subject is too broad and too complex for that. However, it is the twofold objective of this chapter and the one to follow: (1) to indicate the chief problem areas of wage administration, and (2) to give a sufficiently detailed analysis so as to show whether these problems are likely to be surmountable. Not only must the more prominent obstacles to implementing a national incomes program of the surplus-shortage type be identified, but avenues must be in evidence by which an administrative authority might overcome expected difficulties. If avenues do not exist, or do not appear to exist, it can only be concluded that there is basis for objection, perhaps substantive, to the wages policy suggested.

What, then, are some of the more prominent objections and problems that are likely to be encountered upon implementation of a national incomes policy program, designed to combat wage-push inflation? How might these objections and problems be overcome? This chapter will center on the problem of data collection and verification.

The following chapter will discuss certain other aspects of the administrative problem: problems of enforcement, bias within the wages authority, etc. Individually, these latter problems are not so large in importance as those of data collection and evaluation. Collectively, they are of utmost importance.

DATA COLLECTION PROBLEMS

The concept of a labor surplus or of a labor shortage is well established in theoretical economics. Indeed, discussion of the consequences of a disequilibrium situation in a particular market is an integral part of supply and demand analysis.

When an economist designates a particular area as one of labor surplus (shortage), the clearly implied belief is that the situation is one of disequilibrium. This could have any of several meanings. Perhaps the most common are that: (1) the wage rate is too low (high) in that the potential return to workers, in the Pareto welfare sense, would be higher (lower) elsewhere; and/or

(2) the level of unemployment is too high (low) in that pressures exist for a wage fall (rise).

A disequilibrium situation so defined could occur for either of two reasons. The time period for adjustment might be insufficient. Knowledge concerning alternative possibilities might be slow to spread.

From a theoretical standpoint, a general analysis of disequilibrium situations, defined as above, which occur either in factor or in product markets is quite useful. It aids in understanding the market mechanism. It helps pinpoint hindrances to the adjustment process, hindrances which might be attacked on the policy level. However, in spite of defects in the market mechanism, the usual conclusion of a study of disequilibrium situations in a market directed economy is that they tend to be self correcting. As a consequence, past emphasis has been on how to improve the functioning of the economy, rather than upon development of criteria which would be useful for appraising how well a particular market was operating.

No doubt the foregoing explains why, on the empirical level, generally speaking nothing more than casual identification of areas of relative labor surplus or shortage usually has been attempted. Such studies as do exist customarily have not attempted the thorough and careful identification and measurement that an anti-inflation incomes policy program would indicate to be necessary. The objectives of the studies often have been quite different from the present ones.[1] The conditions under which they have

1. An example of this would be the method of measuring "depressed areas," employed by the *Area Redevelopment Act*, Public Law 87-27, 87th Cong., 1st Sess., 1961. Under this act, which is still continuing, but now suffers from lack of funds, the concept of a depressed area is one the government employs to indicate areas of relative labor surplus. The purpose, of course, is to designate areas worthy of Federal assistance. Clearly, then, an immediate difference between the approach of the Act and the approach necessary for a wage control proposal that has an anti-inflation intent is that under the Redevelopment Act no effort is made to indicate areas of relative labor shortage and work to eliminate these situations also. In addition several other distinctions between the procedures adopted by the Area Redevelopment Act and the requirements of an anti-inflation wage control program may be observed. (1) Since measurement of a labor surplus area is a difficult task, and satisfactory objective criteria are difficult to find, the Act places much the greater reliance upon measured unemployment, as the least controversial criterion. Where measured unemployment occurs in amounts adequate to meet the test of "depressed area" the degree of underemployment is not considered relevant by the Act. (2) That section of the Act which deals with "underemployment" fails to meet three

been made differ greatly from those suggested by a wage control framework. They are studies of unregulated markets rather than of regulated markets.

J. C. R. Dow and L. A. Dicks-Mireaux, for example, attempted a fairly exact measurement of excess demand for Great Britain.[2] Their findings were that job vacancies, when correlated with measured unemployment were a reliable ordinal indicator of excess demand. Job vacancies did not show up so well as a cardinal indicator. The closeness of the correlation between measured job vacancies and measured unemployment which Dow and Dicks-Mireaux found led them to have greater confidence in both measures. However, Dow and Dicks studied unregulated markets where no economic incentive to bias the results existed. This would not be the case where policy makers held down the wage bill by artificial means, as would be the case if wage controls to restrain wage-push inflation existed. As an additional difficulty, Dow and Dicks concentrated on job vacancies and measured unemployment,

---

requirements necessary to wage controls with an anti-inflation purpose. Underemployment apparently is considered equivalent to a low wage and is independent of any survey of worker and employer preferences for work and for workers. Aid must be apportioned to all states in equal amounts instead of on the basis of relative need. The total aid available for assistance to underemployment areas has been modest in amount and not adjustable on the administrative level to conform to relative intensity of national need, on a cyclical basis for example. (3) At present a cut-off point exists. Either an area qualifies under the Act or it does not. Further, there is no *legislated* effort to indicate intensity of regional or industrial need and scale aid on that basis. (4) Areas that do not apply for aid do not get it. (5) For the most part, aid is designed to be made available on a geographical basis. Thus, the aid is likely to be of a general sort in that it provides alternate employment opportunities without adequate regard to whether the skills needed are the skills available. (6) Little attention is devoted to the question of whether the wisest adjustment to correct a labor surplus is to shift labor out of the area, or shift employment opportunities into the area.

Finally, in some cases, the aid might perpetuate a disequilibrium situation in the labor market. A "too high" wage could be the result of excessive wage demands which were made in error in the sense that labor did not realize that the market would judge the demands excessive. In this case, the presence of unemployment would be a signal to corrective action. Federal aid which absorbed the unemployment would destroy this as a signal of inappropriate wage policy, and would increase the likelihood that inappropriate wage policies would continue. An incomes program with an anti wage inflation purpose, by contrast, would suggest policy makers react in a very different way. Labor surplus areas should have a wage decrease, not Federal assistance.

2. "The Excess Demand for Labour. A Study of Conditions in Great Britain: 1946-56," *Oxford Economic Papers*, February, 1958, pp. 1-34.

neither of which show degree of underemployment. But measurement of underemployment is a crucial feature of any anti-inflation wage control program, for it is essential to the calculation of degree of relative labor surplus (shortage) market by market.

Thus, in the suggestion that the concept of labor surplus (shortage) be adopted as the primary guide to wage adjustment, reliance is placed upon an old tool in economic analysis. But both the conditions under which the information is to be collected and the character of the information needed are altered. Careful and systematic measurement of the amount of labor surplus (shortage) is recommended now, not just for the economy as a whole, but for each individual labor market as well. On the other side, internal firm data might be available under the controls, which typically have not been available heretofore; and this would ease the measurement task somewhat. In other words, part of the problem of definition of a labor shortage (surplus) which has existed in the past, and might not be so severe given the wage control plan here considered, is that of finding generally available data that would "hint" at the true labor market conditions in a particular situation. That is, many past writers on the concept of a labor shortage (surplus) have considered criteria which would not be appropriate in the present instance, if internal firm data were available.[3]

In an assessment of the problems of data collection and evaluation associated with measurement of labor surplus and shortage in the context of the present work, it is evident that close comparisons with past efforts to accomplish similar ends is not possible.[4] Few such efforts exist. In any event, the conditions under which past studies might have been made would be inadequate, as conclusions reached through a survey of an unregulated economy

3. See, for example, Kenneth Boulding, "An Economist's View of the Manpower Concept," *A Policy for Scientific and Professional Manpower* (New York: National Manpower Council, 1963), pp. 11-32; Dael Wolfle, *America's Resources of Specialized Talent* (New York: Harper and Bros., 1954); David M. Blank and George J. Stigler, *The Demand and Supply of Scientific Manpower* (New York: National Bureau of Economic Research, 1956); A. A. Alchian, K. J. Arrow, and W. M. Capron, *An Economic Analysis of the Market for Scientists and Engineers* (Santa Monica: The Rand Corporation, 1958); and W. Lee Hansen, "The Economics of Scientific and Engineering Manpower," *The Journal of Human Resources*, Spring, 1967, pp. 191-215.

4. In particular it should be noted that while the current wage guideposts do contain reference to labor shortage and labor surplus markets as mentioned in Chapter 8 no real attempt has been made to modify the general 3.2 to 3.5 wage guidepost in specific market applications.

would be applicable to the case of a regulated economy only after substantial evaluation and analysis.

Appraisal of problems which would arise if an incomes policy truly were employed in anti wage-push ways to combat wage inflation must be highly speculative. This speculation must be in two stages. (1) Is it likely that, in spite of his best efforts, a wages administrator would be misled by the wage data collected? (2) Are errors likely to be so great as to induce administrators to strive towards establishment of a pattern of wage rates inferior to that customary in the absence of any intervention by the government?

The first and most obvious statistical problem, which analysis of an incomes policy program appropriately based on the surplus-shortage principle should elicit, is the comprehensive nature of the fact gathering operation. Up-to-date statistics on the number of people available for work in each labor market, whether they were already employed elsewhere or not, would need to be collected. Also necessary would be statistics on job opportunities, *i.e.*, the number of jobs employers would like to fill if qualified workers were available at the market wage. Unfortunately, the need for such data raises a host of procedural questions.

As a first important question, how does one define a labor market?[5] What, for example, is the labor market for grade 2 machinists for an opening with XYZ Co., in their Decatur, Alabama, branch? What are the exact employment needs of XYZ Co.? The only completely unambiguous answer to these questions is that individual market experiments must be conducted to determine issues of this kind. This is not feasible and, of course, not necessary. Perfection is not the goal. A system of allocation as good as that used at present will suffice. However, this does suggest the problems involved should the individual market experiment approach be adopted in principle.

A less utopian alternative would be to generalize and interrelate such factors as: (1) the state of the market for machinists generally, (2) workers' preferences for manufacturing companies of XYZ's general size characteristics, and (3) the labor market situation in Decatur and its environs.

5. For the moment the analysis concentrates upon the task of defining a labor market and measuring the relative labor surplus (shortage) existing therein. The issue of how frequently these measurements should be made and, if infrequently, during what phase of the business cycle, is treated in Chapter 10.

Reliance upon these criteria only would depend upon a number of implicit assumptions, which might be vitiating. Machinists' preferences for manufacturing work do not differ in any significant degree from the preferences of other labor groups. The supply of, relative to the demand for, machinists in Decatur is no different from the supply of, relative to the demand for, labor in that area generally. XYZ Co. is a typical company. Machinists regard it as typical. Finally, machinists in the Decatur area, or machinists likely to be attracted to Decatur at a relevant wage, are no different in their tastes and preferences for work, and in their work capacities, from machinists generally. These assumptions are contrary to fact. Their use detracts from the reliability of the results.

The policy maker now has a choice. A wage determination system, however inadequately executed, which gives separate consideration to the labor needs of every employer, for every job code, as well as separate consideration to the employment preferences of every worker and every potential worker, is one possibility. A wage determination system which summarizes, groups, and standardizes the analysis by means of worker and job evaluation techniques is another possibility.

But the issue is clear. Standardization of wages according to a limited number of generalized criteria is not economically ideal. The only justification for wage administration policy so oriented would be the belief that: (1) standardization of wages would not result in a pattern of wages significantly inferior to those presently existing; and (2) administratively, wage standardization would be enough simpler to warrant the change. Both of these propositions are open to considerable question. The less one is open to question the more is the other.

On balance the U.S. economy has been moving toward greater standardization for some time.[6] But wages still are not very thoroughly standardized. Particularly non-standard are inter-industry and geographical wage differentials. Wage differentials within these two categories follow a more logical pattern. And there is no reason to suppose unregulated wages in the U.S. economy ever would achieve a high degree of standardization. In a theoretical

6. See, for example, Lloyd G. Reynolds and Cynthia H. Taft, *The Evolution of Wage Structure* (New Haven: Yale University Press, 1956), esp. pp. 318-51; or Martin Segal, "Regional Wage Differences in Manufacturing in the Postwar Period," *Review of Economics and Statistics*, May, 1961, pp. 148-55.

utopia, it becomes clear that they should not be standardized.[7]

On the other hand, some argue that a great deal of wage standardization would represent an improvement over existing wage patterns. The reasoning is that too often existing differentials are the result of differing degrees of monopolistic or monopsonistic power in the labor market, rather than of differing work environments and differing job requirements. Therefore, it can be contended, a strong move towards wage standardization would not be any more harmful to patterns of resource allocation than market determined wages. This whole issue is unsettled.

With regard to the relative difficulty of administering a system of individually tailored wages, vis-à-vis a system of standardized wages, there is little question but what wage standardization would simplify the data collection process. Whether or not practical criteria for wage standardization would make the data collection process enough simpler to warrant that approach again is a moot question. Even under such a program of wage standardization much detailed administrative work would remain. Decisions still would need to be made as to workers' true skills and abilities and as to employers' true employment needs.[8]

Whether wage standardization or an administratively more complicated wage program is attempted, the data collection task will be extensive. If the wages authority is charged with full and complete responsibility for data collection and data interpretation, it will be necessary to endow it with many of the attributes of a personnel office. The authority will need to determine when a vacancy exists, and a vacancy of what sort. It also will need to determine when an applicant is qualified to fill a prescribed opening. Clearly this commits the wage authority to a great deal of detailed effort, an activity for which it is not likely to be well suited.

Yet if the government does not assume direct and intimate concern with the employment process, private sources must be

7. For the purposes of this study, this is defined as wages set where marginal revenue product and average cost of acquisition of labor schedules intersect.

8. A partial understanding of the job evaluation problem which a wages administrator would face can be seen from the steel industry's effort to classify something over 180,000 different jobs. See, for example, Jack Stieber, *The Steel Industry Wage Structure. A Study of the Joint Union-Management Job Evaluation Program in the Basic Steel Industry* (Cambridge: Harvard University Press, 1959).

The steel study is not an exact parallel. The study is of just one industry.

relied upon to furnish employment data. But if this course of action is followed, the data so acquired become a great deal more suspect.

"BIAS" IN THE RAW DATA

This brings the analysis to the problem of possible perversion of ends, aims, and/or administrative techniques of the regulatory agency through conscious or unconscious introduction of a bias in the raw data. If it is assumed that the only reasonable administrative possibility is to rely on private sources to supply the necessary "raw" data, how is the regulatory authority to guard against "errors" in the input data?

That the work of data collection needs to be carefully done with assurance that when required, firms report their employment activities promptly and completely, etc., seems so obvious that further discussion of the point ought to be superfluous. However, a bias in collected employment statistics also may arise because of: (1) those who do not bother to make an employment application; (2) those who apply for more than one job; (3) the practice of hoarding workers; (4) artificial restriction of supply of workers by any labor group, organized or unorganized; or (5) an attempt either by labor, or management, singly or collectively, to falsify or otherwise allow their bias to affect reported statistics.

Certainly it would fall to the wages authority to verify whatever statistics were reported to it. In this connection spot sampling might seem useful. Spot samples could be used to determine, in at least an approximate fashion, whether or not an investigation on a larger scale was warranted in a given instance. Naturally a check of this sort would be approximate only, and some things are easier to verify than others. But are all aspects of the data collection process of a sort that could be checked to a greater or lesser extent?

If a firm were to report the number of applicants for a given opening it should be relatively easy to verify this if names were taken. If names were not taken, the firm should not be allowed a wage reduction on the basis of its claims alone. With regard, how-

---

It was made by management and labor working together. Were a government administrator to attempt the same task, it would be much more difficult.

ever, to verification of those who applied, but whose applications were not reported by the firm, this group could be estimated only by some sort of sampling process, by unemployment records, by direct appeal for said applicants to present themselves to a local wages administrator or by some combination of these techniques.

If the applications for a particular job were reported, but not counted because the applicant was considered unqualified, a check of this would be most difficult. Many value judgments are involved in determining whether someone would make a desirable employee. Those who did apply, but whose applications were not counted, would be the hardest group to estimate both as to size and as to work qualifications.

Determination of how many applications are a duplication, or not altogether serious, such as those from persons who are trying merely to find out if they could get a given job, as well as how many available workers simply did not bother to apply, is largely a job of estimating. It could be done by the wage authority or by private individuals. It might be best if the wage authority compiled these estimates. This would save much duplication of effort. Hence the government could afford to do a more careful job here than could any one employer.

The tasks of data collection and of data evaluation that have been outlined are exceedingly broad and complex. Thus far the only device suggested to help restrict their magnitude has been the technique of sampling. Moreover, the sampling job would involve more than mere counting of noses. The type of sampling needed would be one which yielded an estimate of unemployment, underemployment, and overemployment (as the case might be) by skill classification, by region, and/or by particular plant opportunities. Quite clearly this is a complex and difficult job.

Data verification via the technique of sampling must be employed judiciously. It is not possible to sample anything and everything and still keep administrative expenses low enough to justify an incomes policy that is even slightly detailed. There is considerable question as to whether sampling will be of enough aid to warrant serious reliance upon it. Sampling is particularly inadequate where the labor market is small or where its bounds are indefinite. What, then, is to be done?

One possibility would be to concentrate solely on those unemployed. If this procedure were followed, it might be theorized, a considerable reduction in the size of the statistical reporting task would be possible. Extensive surveys of employed workers no longer would be needed, instead interest could focus just on those out of work, a comparatively small portion of the labor force. Of course, this is a portion that is subject to a good deal of variation in size over a period of time, but this should not complicate the analysis too much. Analysis only of the unemployed has the additional advantage that large numbers of statistics concerning this group already are being gathered, much of which would be helpful to a wages administrator.

There are two serious difficulties with concentrating solely on unemployed workers. One is that existing statistical procedures concentrate on estimating the total number of unemployed. Estimates by skill classification or by geographical distribution are done on a more casual basis. This would have to be corrected. That would involve a significant increase in data collection work, and it would require definition of a skill, and of a geographical area. Studies of worker mobility also would be helpful, but perhaps not quite so essential. Correct forecast of labor mobility would facilitate a more correct first estimate of labor surplus (shortage). However, if first estimates of mobility were incorrect, this might be rectified by subsequent recommendations for changes in relative wage rates. It would depend upon the practicality of successive approximation as a technique for the establishment of equilibrium wage rates. By contrast, if measurement or definition of workers' skills or geographical displacement were incorrect, the successive approximation process would not mitigate the failure. The guide to adjustments would be permanently in error, because the employment data upon which recommended wage changes must be based would be false.

A second difficulty with concentrating solely on unemployed workers is of even greater concern. Present estimates of unemployment devote little attention to disguised unemployment, to those workers who are in some sense underemployed. This procedure is both inadequate and near impossible to correct. The seriousness of the difficulty can be illustrated by a hypothetical example.

Assume a decrease in the demand for skilled machinists. In such a situation some skilled machinists would move into jobs rated for semi-skilled workers. If this movement is fairly prompt and relatively uninhibited, the result would be displacement of workers who were truly semi-skilled. These then become the men unemployed. In this instance analysis of the skills of the unemployed would indicate a surplus of semi-skilled machinists and a need for a decline in the wage of this group. This is a part of the desired adjustment to a shift in the demand for the skilled machinist. But it is only a part. What may not be so obvious, from a study solely of those unemployed, is the coincidental need for a decline in the wages of skilled machinists. And the successive approximation adjustment process is no aid. If the skills of those employed as semi-skilled are not appraised, no change in the wage of skilled machinists will be indicated as necessary. Economic forces working to correct the situation will not exist. Clearly, the wages authority cannot study only those unemployed. Their concern also must be with those underemployed.[9]

At this juncture the definitional problem again is encountered. How can it be determined if a worker is underemployed? Exactly how underemployed is he? Then too, once the door is opened for consideration of the underemployed, an earlier problem reappears. It is not possible for a wage authority to verify every employee, actual or prospective, as to his true qualifications. It is not possible for a wage authority to verify every job opening, filled or unfilled, as to exactly what skills are required. Again the question, how can these statistical tasks be simplified? Can they be simplified?

As a second possible way to simplify the data collection and evaluation task, suppose the wages authority were to confine its

9. This observation also seems relevant to employment experiences in unregulated markets. A study of those unemployed almost invariably indicates that a disproportionately large percentage are in the unskilled or semi-skilled category.

For the individual the diagnosis is clear—acquire a marketable skill. Many, however, go on to assume that the prescription for the economy is equally clear—there is no longer much need for the unskilled or semi-skilled worker. See, for example, "The Labor Market in Mid-1961," *Federal Reserve Bulletin*, June, 1961, pp. 647-53.

But analysis suggests that whatever unemployment exists, be it frictional or the result of a general deficiency in aggregate monetary demand, logically ought to consist of a high percentage in the least skilled categories, and this is so regardless of the general skill level of the nation's work force. Alternatively phrased, this means that higher education for workers may increase their mobility slightly but in general it will not solve the problem of national unemployment; and technological change both can and will adapt to the work force, whatever its character. Over time, innovations can be expected to be primarily labor saving, or capital saving, depending upon the dictates of the market.

activities solely to recommending the wage level for a particular plant or business. Labor and management then could settle the exact dispersion of wage rates between themselves. All of these decisions would be made entirely within the firm. The problem here, however, is that of determining the average wage appropriate. The wage authority would not be able to do this unless and until it knew the relative intensity of need for workers in each skill classification. Stated more exactly the wages authority would need a formula by which relative need might be expressed. This is necessary if the individual firm is going to be allowed to adjust the input mix to take best advantage of relative input prices. It is necessary because as relative prices change so will the relative intensity of need for input factors.

As still another approach to simplification of the task of data collection and evaluation, would it be possible to establish a general set of working rules by which the policy maker could determine where bias in the raw data was most likely to occur? That is, what groups have the greatest economic interest in distorting the data? If this were known, perhaps it would be possible to simplify the administrative task. The policy maker would know where to concentrate data verification efforts. As an additional advantage, the policy maker would have, in those areas that did not have a strong economic incentive to bias the raw data, a standard or norm by which to judge those that did.

It should be noted at this point that mere presence of incentive to bias the data does not guarantee that bias will occur, only that the likelihood of bias is increased. Further, any bias which is introduced might be introduced consciously, but also it might be introduced unconsciously. In fact, an unconscious bias seems the more likely. It derives from the differing motives of employee, employer, and policy maker. The individual employer wants capable help at a modest wage. The individual employee wants a desirable job at a good wage. The policy maker wants a high level of employment and an economical pattern of resource allocation. These partially opposing objectives can lead to divergent evaluations as to adequacy of worker skills and job requirements. The evaluation may be honestly meant nonetheless. However, from the standpoint of determining a theoretically correct wage, it makes little difference if the bias is consciously or unconsciously introduced. In either case the amount of "error" must be estimated, and a correction factor must then be subsequently introduced.

Investigation of economic motives for introducing a bias into employment statistics, given anti wage-push controls and wage inflation, indicates that they usually are present. Some of these motives relate to imperfectly competitive markets only. Others relate to all markets. Some do not depend upon degree of market perfection at all but upon institutional practices. To investigate these motives, the analysis will consider the probable behavior of business and of labor in several different situations.

On the employers' side of the market, other things remaining equal, any firm faced with a rising supply curve of labor would profit through maintaining a level of employment and of wages below that where marginal revenue product and the average cost of labor acquisition schedules intersect. On the employees' side of the market, by contrast, if labor operates as any other monopolist then it would attempt to reduce the level of employment, so as to force the wage rate up, whenever the demand for labor was down-sloping. Thus, whenever an imperfect market exists, so too does motive for deviation from the "optimum" wage.[10] This does not mean either group necessarily would capitalize upon its market position to influence the wage rate, but this possibility always is present. Further, the greater the slope of the curves the stronger the incentive to bias the data.

Motive for bias thus exists practically everywhere. But since most labor markets are reasonably competitive, often the motive is weak and deviation from the optimum therefore probably would be slight. With this in mind, the policy maker well might decide to concentrate data evaluation efforts on the very imperfect markets. Indeed this is the only sensible course of action. It does, however, raise some problems of its own. How imperfect is imperfect? What is the degree of slope of labor supply and demand, by skill classification, by geographical area, by industry, etc.? This, in turn, involves problems of definition of a labor market earlier described. That is, what are the proper skill, area, firm, and industry boundaries to a labor market?

Thus far, however, the analysis has assumed that firms at least act *as if* to maximize profits and that labor behaves no dif-

10. The reader is reminded that this book's definition of the micro optimum is where the marginal revenue product and average cost of acquisition of labor schedules intersect. *Supra*, pp. 98-100.

ferently from any other monopolist. Neither of these assumptions is particularly realistic. This is especially true of the labor side of the market.[11] But if other goals, either economic or non-economic, are pursued, the analysis no longer will apply. In instances of this sort the policy maker would have to rely on historical experience, and on the tools of institutional economics generally, to indicate these other motives. In those cases where motivation results from efforts to achieve a multiplicity of goals, it would be necessary to determine which of these goals and motivations were the important ones, and to determine the relative strength of the more important of these goals and motivations. All this seems pretty impractical, but there is more.

For all markets, economic incentive for introducing a bias in the raw data exists whenever the aggregate wage is not an equilibrium one. This is true for competitive markets as well as for imperfectly competitive markets. It also is true for those markets where standard monopoly and monopsony models apply and for those where these models do not apply.

In a situation of over-full employment, all firms have an economic incentive to raise their effective wage, and labor to cooperate. If a situation of less than full employment exists, firms have an economic incentive to work for a wage lower than otherwise would occur. Labor also might cooperate in this objective in the interest of facilitating, in each individual market situation, the highest possible level of employment.

The above thus demonstrates, again, that the way in which macro wage policies are structured, and the success achieved in their implementation, is relevant to the problem of micro-economic wage regulation. It reinforces, with another example, the general point made much earlier that there is a close tie-in between micro and macro wage policy and between wage policy and the general economic environment.

To illustrate this particular relationship in somewhat greater detail, assume that policy makers select an employment goal which is equivalent to over-full employment in the Ohlin sense. All markets then will have an economic incentive to bias the data, but not all markets will respond with equal intensity. Further, not all

11. John T. Dunlop, *Wage Determination Under Trade Unions* (New York: Augustus M. Kelley, Inc., 1950), pp. 28-44, suggests some more realistic possibilities.

attempts to bias wage data will be equally successful. Herein lies the core of the micro problem. A policy effort to maintain, for example, a situation of over-full employment will manifest itself in part through additional problems for micro-economic wage regulation and through additional micro-economic inadequacies.

In view of the above, a next logical question is: to what extent is it likely that the selected macro objective would provide micro problems? One aspect of the issue already has been treated. Chapter 7 discussed problems inherent in the selection of specific macro-economic wage targets, given the selected objective of high employment. The conclusion was that imperfections in achieving the stated goal are a certainty, and that these imperfections could be even greater than those to be found in the absence of regulation. Aside from this, there is another problem which may be even more significant.

If pressures for inappropriate wage increases are at the root of the inflation problem, if the wage inflation thesis is valid, then in one sense anti wage-push controls are designed to yield over-full employment. Thus, the possibility is postulated that the macro goal selected would provide intense regulatory problems on the micro-economic level. Pressures for wage increases could exist in all markets, and they could be fairly strong.

Given the wage inflation thesis, whether or not upward wage pressures would exist in all markets and their relative strength, would depend upon the specific character of the wage inflation process. As shown in Chapter 3 and also in Chapter 5, the wage inflation thesis need not assume all labor markets equally culpable. The union wage inflation thesis is an example. Here the assumption is that only the unionized sector is initially at fault for excessive upward wage pressures.

Even if the breadth of the wage inflation experience could be established, its relative intensity and difficulty of eradication still would be open to question. For example, if spontaneous wage increases simply are starters for an inflationary round, then upward wage pressures might be relatively mild, and presumably more easily controlled. Certainly they would be milder in this case, than if wage increases in the culpable sector did not induce equivalent percentage increases elsewhere in the economy.

Another point to consider is the general psychology of wage inflation. Heretofore, a primary emphasis of inflation theory has been on which sector is at fault, without equivalent concern as to why the guilty sector behaves as it does. Perhaps, for example, labor leaders feel they are in a competitive race for money wage increases, which they must obtain or lose the support of their membership.[12] If this is so, a national incomes policy easily might eradicate the problem. Union leaders then could shift any blame for their failure to obtain money wage increases onto the government regulators. On the other hand, if, in spite of wage controls, labor remains preoccupied with money wage increases, the problem of coping with wage inflation pressures may be much more difficult.

Clearly the job of selecting the labor market most needful of scrutiny by the wage authority is a difficult one. The choice depends upon many factors, but the issue of inflation cause is particularly relevant. Should that phase of the administrative task which deals with selection of the labor market needful of scrutiny be surmounted, other problems remain. As implied earlier, a study would have to be made in these markets to indicate not only the true number of job applications, but the true qualifications of these applicants as well.

But suppose a dispute arose as to the quality of a given job applicant or of a given job. In such cases judgment would be required to determine whether the applicant was indeed qualified, or the job as difficult, or as easy, as claimed. It might be hoped that these issues could be resolved satisfactorily on the basis of what the firm had done in the past, what other firms are doing, or some other such comparative criteria. In actual practice, it seems unlikely that a workable set of criteria exists upon which to base such answers. Which of several criteria should be used?[13]

To obviate the above dilemma the only alternative is for the wages administrator to rely most heavily on employer supplied data, union supplied data, or some combination of the two. In practice,

12. This sort of problem relates to the political aspects of trade union leadership activity and is discussed at length by Arthur Ross in his book *Trade Union Wage Policy*.

13. Experiences with Fair Employment Practices Commission activities on the state level are further indication of the magnitude of this problem. The Civil Rights Act of 1964 may present another illustration. Certainly, as of the time of this writing, enforcement under the Act is off to an impressive beginning, but one wonders if enforcement will be so simple or so dramatic in its accomplishments when those who do not wish to comply begin to practice somewhat greater subtlety in their methods of non-compliance. Outright defiance is easier to combat than unspoken but nonetheless active opposition.

it seems probable that the larger emphasis would have to be on employer supplied data. On occasion the wage authority might modify the claims of employers, but three strong objections would prevent their going to the other extreme of working exclusively on the basis of union claims.

In the first place, it seems doubtful if the general public would be willing to accept unions as sufficiently responsible to be charged with much wage setting responsibility. And there is some justification for this position. Even apart from the exercise of monopoly power from time to time, too often union leaders seek differentials of pay on the basis of skill, of seniority, of craft, of job requirements, or of geographical area, which are not in accord with market conditions, but instead seem to conform to an abstract concept of wage justice in some sort of Aquinas sense.

In the second place, it is the employer who compiles the bulk of the data. It is the employer who collects cost information. It is the employer, working through a personnel office, who has the bulk of the preliminary contacts with the labor market.[14] And it is the employer who collects whatever data exist that bear on marginal revenue productivity.

In the third place, as demonstrated by the wage inflation thesis, unions may have an especial bias towards inflationary wage increases. If the objectives of high full employment and price-level stability are to be served, this bias must not be allowed to influence wage policy. An obvious way to accomplish this is not to rely upon labor groups for wage data. The extent to which this suggestion ought to be relied upon in practice, of course, would depend in part upon the particular characteristics of the wage inflation thesis assumed to be relevant.

The possibility of a compromise between employer claims and union claims also offers limited hope of being a real improvement. Sooner or later one is brought to the inevitable question—in the event of a conflict, whom to accept, labor or management. Short of an exhaustive investigation by the wages authority as a means of ascertaining all the facts through independent effort, primary reliance upon employer supplied data seems wisest. Even with a wages authority investigation, an initial predisposition towards employer supplied data seems only prudent.

14. This would not be as true where a closed shop, or a practical equivalent thereof, existed.

Chapter 10

IMPLEMENTATION OF THE CONTROL PROPOSAL: OTHER ADMINISTRATIVE PROBLEMS

THUS FAR THE CONCLUSION as to the efficacy of a national incomes policy seriously and universally employed as the main policy tool for wage inflation control is that precise administrative criteria are lacking in crucial situations. It is true that in some cases (purely competitive markets or a very close real-world approximate) the appropriate criteria are present. They would work so long as the aggregate demand for labor was equated to the aggregate supply. In other cases (mildly imperfect markets) the available criteria still can be expected to yield workable results in the sense that deviation from the competitive case will be slight, again provided there is not excess aggregate demand for labor.

But the question of what ought to be the wage in an imperfectly competitive labor market, or the wage in any market when there is excess demand for labor, is a problem of a different sort. This is particularly troublesome because these are precisely the conditions under which the argument for an incomes policy is the strongest. Further, the more imperfect the labor market, or the greater the excess demand for labor, the more acute the problem of selecting an appropriate wage becomes.

In imperfect labor markets economic incentive to bias the data exists. Investigation in these situations would be required to ascertain if the established wage were economically appropriate under the national incomes policy criteria developed, and, if not, what sort of adjustment should be recommended. Conceivably the investigative task necessary to such a judgment might be accomplished by measuring, as best as can be done, marginal revenue product and average cost of acquisition of labor for various classes of workers in various labor situations. The data derived then could be employed to determine, where necessary, optimum skill requirements for different jobs, and optimum wages for these skills in the jobs in which they will be used. But this is a possibility that is implicit in any textbook discussion of wage theory and long has proved impractical in administration by government. If national incomes policy to combat wage inflation is to offer any sort of positive contribution, it must be to suggest some other approach. Comparison with other markets, where the wage is properly determined, is one alternative.

In the absence of pressures on aggregate demand, a possible basis for comparison does exist. When there is no excess demand for labor, competitive markets would be expected to determine wages in an appropriate way. Thus comparisons might be made between imperfect and competitive labor markets. But, as earlier indicated, no unique set of comparative criteria exists that reasonably could be expected to function as an administrative bench mark. This raises the question, in any given situation what comparisons are the appropriate comparisons?

Where excess aggregate demand for labor exists, which is being maintained by accident or by policy design, even comparative criteria are likely to be absent. Such a situation could be the result of a conscious policy to perpetuate over-full employment in the Ohlin sense. The possibility that this would occur, particularly if the wage inflation hypothesis is assumed correct, was discussed in Chapter 9. However, a condition of over-full employment also might be the result of an attempt to maintain full employment more or less continuously. Here over-full employment could be an accident in that it results from over-caution, but it is an accident that continually recurs. Another possible explanation for a perpetuated disequilibrium situation of this kind would be that the regulatory authority misjudged the amount of frictional unemployment that was "normal."

Where over-full employment is present, all firms, regardless of market structure, will have an economic motive for attempting to obtain a level of wages other than that which a wages authority in possession of full knowledge, and operating according to the criteria described in Chapter 8, would prescribe. In these situations, actions by individual firms, often in cooperation with their employees, too frequently will be in conflict with national policies.

Should they so desire, possible means by which firms might thwart the desires of the regulatory authority are legion. These means include: secret adjustments in rates of pay (bonuses or penalties); adjustments of an efficiency wage;[1] adjustment of hours of work (particularly of work that involves an overtime premium); upgrading (downgrading) of rank or skill classification; etc. Other somewhat more extreme measures also exist. Possibilities include the transfer of workers to salaried occupations, if those are not covered, or the subcontracting of work to individual "entrepreneurs," much as is done now in the case of newspaper delivery boys.

From the analysis of the administrative problems of wage rate regulation, it is evident that objective criteria for wages control either are lacking or else much too difficult to measure. This does not mean that a given wage always will be inappropriate. Neither must it mean that most wages will be inappropriate, although the probability certainly would be in that direction. It does mean, however, that the amount and frequency of inaccuracy in wages over the nation will depend in no small part upon how the wages authority goes about its task. Since objective criteria are not present, the composition of the wages authority is of great concern because latitude for judgment must, of necessity, be considerable.

National incomes policy needs to achieve a pattern of wages at least as good as those in an unregulated market, but with a level of wages different from what otherwise would occur. To accomplish this, the wages authority would first need to ascertain, from available statistics, a reasonable approximation of the true supply and demand conditions existing in each market. Such estimates call for skilled judgment combined with a large element of

1. This quite frequently is easy to accomplish. If workers are on a time wage, increase their work load. If they are on an efficiency wage, the wage bill will need to be adjusted. Techniques here are ones with which many workers already are well acquainted. Perhaps the most common means is to restudy or redesign the job, and at the same time adjust the workers' "norm" in such a way as to effect a wage change. Probably the most convenient time to restudy a job is when a new machine is introduced.

good fortune. If the true goals of members of the wages authority are other than wages based on competitive criteria, the resulting entanglement is likely to be nearly hopeless.

Unfortunately, chances that the wages authority would be sufficiently biased to accept some adulteration of the competitive concept seem fairly good. There are several reasons why this is so. In the first place, the likelihood of an administrative group that is biased to begin with seems strong. All too often there is a tendency to appoint representatives from each of the interested groups in approximately equal numbers. In this case, the expectation would be to have representatives from the side of labor, from the side of management, and an "impartial" group designed to represent the public.[2] And, even if the committee approach is not used, reference to the views and feelings of these groups in the process of arriving at wage decisions is common. Such a procedure introduces a bias at the very outset since the only group which should be served is the public sector.

Another reason why the wages authority may begin with a biased attitude flows from difficulty in finding adequate personnel. It is hard to find persons who are technically qualified and familiar with the industry in question, but who are not employees, former employees, or prospective future employees of the industry they are to regulate. Moreover this problem is not one that is encountered only at the highest administrative level. The problem applies equally to the lower echelon governmental servant, upon whose judgment and discovery of reliable facts so much ultimately depends.

Apart from any initial predispositions on the part of regulatory personnel, an administrative bias also is likely to result from the very nature of the regulatory activity. It is typical of regulatory agencies, whether formally constructed or not, that they tend to sympathize with the areas they regulate. This sympathetic attitude could take any of several forms.

A bias in favor of raising the wages of low wage groups is a likely possibility. As one example, this bias is reflected in the widely prevalent belief that low wages are the result of economic exploitation, somehow defined, although available evidence indicates the

2. The regulatory boards charged with wages administration in the U. S. during World War I, World War II, and the Korean conflict were all of this tripartite character.

contrary.[3] Another possible manifestation of a sympathetic attitude by the regulatory authority for the group regulated would be
reflected in a desire to help perpetuate industries or skills that
otherwise would be adjudged unnecessary by the economic system.
State laws which unnecessarily restrict the use of large and efficient
commercial fishing methods exemplify this. Efforts to perpetuate
the family farm sometimes represent another manifestation. A
sympathetic attitude also may be expressed in the form of a reluctance to reduce the money wage, the real wage, or perhaps even
the relative share of income going to a particular sector. Efforts to
maintain "traditional" wage differentials in the face of economic
pressure to the contrary would be an example.

Under the present U.S. wage guideposts, as another illustration,
these expectations apparently are fulfilled again. Data are not
complete enough for exact evaluation, but there seems a tendency to
allow labor the benefit of every doubt both in the calculation of
degree of labor shortage, market by market, and in the establishment of allowable "productivity" wage increases designed to be
standard over the nation.

In short, it is to be expected that wage administrators would
be subject to the usual faults associated with a regulatory agency.[4]
Whether these attitudes would result in macro-economic complications in the form of a too high wage level as well is difficult to
say. This has been the history of wage regulation during wartime,
and it also seems to be in evidence elsewhere.

In the United States, World War I is a particularly dramatic
demonstration of a wartime failure. Breakdown of the World War
II "hold the line order" also is an example. Only in World War II
was the need for a "non-inflationary" level of wages clearly established as a prime goal for the wage authority. But a non-inflationary wage level was not achieved in either situation.

Study of regulated wages in under-developed nations discloses
macro-economic failings in quite a different context. Here again
there seems a tendency for all wages to be too high. The general
philosophy in these countries seems to be: "wage justice," prevent-

3. Gordon F. Bloom, "A Reconsideration of the Theory of Exploitation,"
Quarterly Journal of Economics, May 1941, pp. 413-42. This article is reprinted
in American Economic Association, *Readings in the Theory of Income Distribution* (Philadelphia: The Blakiston Company, 1951), pp. 245-77.

4. For a discussion of these faults, see Marver Bernstein, *Regulating Business by Independent Commission* (Princeton: Princeton University Press, 1955).

ing "exploitation," helping workers at the expense of capitalists, etc.[5]

The intent of national incomes criteria must be that relative increases in wage differentials would be offset by relative decreases. But this objective might not be realized in practice. The earlier discussed concepts of ability to pay, comparative wages, minimum budgets, and productivity (in the output per worker sense) seem to underlie much "lay" thinking about how proper wages ought to be determined. In those markets where the wage authority is called upon for judgment, these ideas may be influential. They are likely to influence if the wage authority does not fully understand and accept the logic of the incomes policy proposal that has been outlined including the general-equilibrium economics, and normative allocation theory upon which the proposal depends.

OTHER ASPECTS OF THE ADMINISTRATIVE PROBLEM

Thus far the discussion of "administrative aspects" of national incomes policy as an anti-inflation device has concentrated primarily upon the problems of data collection and data verification. Unquestionably these are among the most complex and difficult issues facing the wage administrator bent upon implementing incomes policy as a companion policy to monetary and fiscal policy for wage inflation control. Nonetheless, there are a number of other administrative questions yet to be discussed. Individually, perhaps, these are not so important as those of data collection and data verification, but collectively they are of extreme importance.

The Administrative Lag. Individual labor markets need to adapt to changing economic conditions. Whether changes in wages could be made promptly enough, given administration involvement in the wage setting process, depends upon ability to forecast needed changes, speed with which a given change influences the economy,

5. P. T. Bauer, "Regulated Wages in Under-Developed Countries," *The Public Stake in Union Power*, ed. Philip D. Bradley (Charlottesville: University of Virginia Press, 1959), p. 34. This study led Bauer to conclude that there is a tendency for all wages to be too high where regulated wages are found. A survey of wage administration in Australia yields the same conclusion for that country. Keith Hancock, "Wages Policy and Price Stability in Australia, 1953-60," *Economic Journal*, September, 1960, pp. 543-60; and Charles E. Rockwood, "National Wage Fixing Arrangements in Australia," *Southern Journal of Business*, October, 1967, pp. 26-37.

frequency of wage change needed to render the adjustment process effective, and procedures used. Inasmuch as ability to forecast often will not be very good, and because of the slowness with which wage changes often influence the economy, administrative promptness is a crucial issue.

If, as one author suggests,[6] where information is needed and the tool for the gathering and interpretation of wage data is that of the Congressional hearing, the lag would be very great indeed. This same problem also seems likely if the courts were relied upon as a "last resort" for wage determination in disputed cases.[7] Indeed, the slowness of these methods would seem to be vitiating.

On the other hand, and under the assumption of pretty general and widely dispersed needs for fact gathering, together with other governmental involvement in the wage setting process, if the idea of regional committees with a good deal of autonomy is followed, perhaps the administrative lag would not be so great as to render ineffective the control program. The proximity of regional committees to particular market situations should facilitate the speed and correctness of administration rulings. Certainly the wisdom of the regional committee idea is supported by U.S. wage regulation experiences during World War II.

As a measure of the magnitude of an administrative lag, our World War II experiences in wage rate regulation seem sufficiently parallel to indicate that the administrative lag would be significant, but perhaps not too great. Exact records on World War II performance were not kept. On the basis of two samples taken late in the war period, however, approximately 60 per cent of the total number of cases were handled in less than six months, something over 10 per cent were handled in less than three months, while about 5 per cent took more than one year to settle. In this connec-

6. Emmette S. Redford, *Potential Public Policies to Deal with Inflation Caused by Market Power*, study paper No. 10, prepared in connection with the study of employment growth, and price levels, U.S. Congress, Joint Economic Committee, 86th Cong., 1st sess., 1959, p. 9.

7. The courts might be used in either of two ways. They might be used as an agency for review of all facts with the aim of recalculating wages set by the regulatory authority, whenever one or more of the parties concerned should request such action. On the other hand the courts might perform much the same function they now do for various quasi-judicial regulatory groups, namely to insure that the duly constituted regulatory authority used fair and legal methods in the course of reaching a decision. Clearly the former would be, in the main, more time consuming than the latter.

tion, the wording on this subject in the *Termination Report of the National War Labor Board* is revealing.[8]

> During its life the Board was frequently criticized by labor, management, and the public on the length of time required in the processing of cases. In the light of the emergency, much of this criticism was understandable and gave the Board considerable concern. There were extenuating circumstances, however, which were not generally appreciated. The most important of these was the process through which a dispute case had to go before the Board could *effectively* and *fairly* consider the issues involved on their merits.

By contrast with the above, however, experiences with the administration of the Walsh-Healy Act, which represents a somewhat similar but much simpler problem, are much less encouraging. The Walsh-Healy Public Contracts Act applies only to those firms on government contract in excess of $10,000. The act is designed to specify minimum wages only. The issue of fringe benefits and of what is economically appropriate is rarely a factor. Primary concern is with what has been "standard" money wage practice in the industry. Yet administration under the act is a time consuming process, and the results often are not satisfying.[9]

Objective criteria for deciding whether to bracket the industry according to finely divided product lines or broad product lines with geographical subdivisions seem lacking. A primary motivation for market classification seems to be the nature and extent of labor and management "exceptions" that are taken to initial rulings or proposed rulings. Partly as a consequence no doubt of lack of objective criteria, and in spite of the relative simplicity of the wage setting task, the time consumed in administering the Walsh-Healy Act is apt to be quite long. For example, a survey of wages in the manufacture of fabricated structural steel was made in March of 1957. The tentative ruling was made in 1959, but as of June, 1962, the final ruling still was pending.

On balance it seems evident that administrative involvement in the wage setting process would tend to cause wage adjustments to be less promptly responsive to changing market conditions than is presently the case. This would not be true in every instance, as

8. Pp. 484-86.
9. C. L. Christenson and R. A. Myren, *Wage Policy under the Walsh-Healy Public Contracts Act* (Bloomington: Indiana University Press, 1966).

there are some possibly disadvantageous aspects of private bargaining over wages that might be avoided. The government would not need to saddle itself with the long-term wage contracts now common. The government would not have to allow the right to strike and therefore perhaps need not go to great lengths to attempt to avoid frequent work stoppages of this kind.

Nonetheless, an administrative lag, while not absolutely certain to occur, does seem likely in most instances. The degree to which such a lag might be a serious drawback to any national wages policy, of course, would be importantly a function of the specific administrative procedures adopted and the funds made available to implement them, as well as how extensive an administrative task was attempted in the first place. In this connection it should be noted that lack of readily obtainable criteria for wage administration would contribute to an administrative lag.

Frequency of Wage Reappraisal. A second problem, which is related to that of the administrative lag, concerns the frequency of relative wage rate adjustments.

The point was established in Chapter 7 that the level of wages must not be subject to too frequent fluctuation. Secular adjustment in the wage level is the appropriate goal. This may be accomplished by gradual and frequent wage adjustment or by periodic and larger incremental wage level changes. The important point is that adjustment in the wage level, and the effects of this adjustment, must be predictable. Given the wage control framework thus far established, neither cyclical adjustment in the level of wages nor frequent revision of secular policies appears a desirable goal. As explained in Chapter 7, such changes would complicate too greatly the task of price stabilizing monetary and fiscal policy as well as wage pattern adjustment.

The general injunction, however, against too frequent wage level changes, leaves open the question of frequency of relative wage rate adjustment as well as the matter of how to encourage gradual and predictable wage-level changes. In a constantly growing and changing economy, there is a need for continual revision of relative wage scales in all sectors. But the amount of change necessary in any particular market would be difficult to predict. Success in prediction would depend upon: correct estimates of present labor supply and demand market by market, correct prediction of the direction and magnitude of future change in each market, and correct prediction of the direction and magnitude of relative wage adjustments needed, in each case, to bring about desired results as well as correct prediction of needed national wage-level adjustments. It is inconceivable that this job of estimation could be done with a high degree of accuracy. But the degree of success which can be expected is important because upon it depends the value of market by market unemployment data as a guide to wage rate adjustment.

The economic consequence of errors of forecast in needed wage changes depends in part upon how frequently corrections, in the form of a revised wage pattern, can be made. This, in turn, depends both upon economic and upon administrative considerations. The preceding section, on the administrative lag, considered issues of administrative feasibility. The outlook was not found promising. It remains for us now to consider economic aspects of this same problem.

Four economic factors cooperate to make too frequent relative wage change a very undesirable thing. First, time is needed for a wage change to induce mobility of workers and employers. It takes time for knowledge of alternate possibilities to spread, and still more time for shifts to be effected. Second, too frequent change in relative wages may destroy whatever effectiveness these wage movements have in inducing factor mobility. For wage differentials to be at all effective in inducing factor mobility they need to have some degree of permanency. Third, too frequent change in relative wages is likely to have a debilitating effect on national productivity as workers strongly oppose a widely fluctuating wage, unless they are provided with a fairly large uncertainty premium.[10] Fourth, too frequent wage change is likely to complicate greatly the task of price stabilizing monetary and fiscal policy. The point already has been discussed at some length in Chapters 6, 7, and 8. As earlier demonstrated, rapid and violent shifts in wage patterns will influence the total of wages paid, price and employment levels. But prices and employment are the variables which were to guide monetary and fiscal adjustments as well as macro-economic wage policy.

10. There is an abundance of evidence to indicate that this is so. Surveys of worker motivation have repeatedly demonstrated that steady employment is of the greatest importance. See, for example, Edwin E. Ghiselli and Clarence W. Brown, *Personnel and Industrial Psychology* (New York: McGraw-Hill Book Company, Inc., 1955), pp. 425-30.

The possibility that price and employment level changes could be largely the result of wage pattern adjustment would destroy the use of these guides as a signal both for macro-economic wage policy and for monetary and fiscal adjustments.

In addition to the above cited difficulties, there is the problem of coordinating wage level and wage pattern adjustments. Given that the wage level objective is to select the wage most compatible with full employment, somehow defined, it then becomes evident that the wage pattern objective must be whatever pattern is most compatible with this wage level. This means that market studies of labor supply and demand as a guide to wage patterns appropriate are completely relevant only if, when studied, the economy is at the target level of employment.

If the economy is experiencing a level of employment either above or below the selected macro target, the market will yield false wage pattern signals. The policy maker thus will need to interpret most labor market data. Interpretative judgment will need to be applied in greater or lesser amounts depending upon: (1) the degree to which the level of employment deviates from the target level, (2) the degree to which this deviation can be expected to affect the labor market in question, and (3) the degree to which leads and lags destroy the validity of market survey data.

With the many objections to frequent adjustment of relative wage rates which are bound to exist, given a national incomes policy aimed at limiting wage inflation, and with the additional complications which cyclical fluctuations in output and employment bring to the task of interpreting labor market data, it is evident that the wage adjustment process discussed is by no means an exact tool and, to the extent that it is useful, it is useful only over a comparatively long period of time. Its precise value would depend, of course, upon a host of factors. These include: ability to achieve macro-economic stability, degree to which inability to achieve macro targets provides micro problems, and facility with which administrative problems are handled. However, it is evident that, when speaking of the frequency of relative wage adjustment that is proper, thinking should be in terms of years rather than weeks or months. An important administrative difficulty then is how to encourage private groups, employers and workers, to forego short-run wage pattern adjustments regarded as potentially damaging to national employment and price-level objectives.

Magnitude of the Wage Change. Under the national incomes policy program outlined, occupational and geographical mobility of workers and of employment opportunities is designed to be encouraged by relative wage rate variation. Accordingly, a formula must be developed by which the wage change for a particular area can be calculated. Such a formula would need to do two things: (1) It would need to identify disequilibrium markets, those for which a wage change was indicated. (2) It would need to measure in disequilibrium situations the wage change appropriate.

A possible formula, certainly, is one that ties employment objectives for particular markets to national employment levels and relates wage changes to the degree of deviation between levels of unemployment in a particular market and levels of national unemployment. As an additional variant, a concession might be made to labor's reluctance to accept money wage decreases under any condition. Absolute wage rate decreases would not be permitted.

In practice this would mean, for example, that a labor market with neither a defined surplus nor shortage of labor would experience a normal wage increase only. That is, the wage would rise by whatever amount the macro criteria indicated to be the appropriate average increase in money wages. A market characterized by a level of unemployment one half the national average, as an example, might receive double the average wage increase until the shortage was corrected. By contrast, workers in a labor market with unemployment twice the national average would not receive even the average incremental increase until the shortage situation corrected itself.

But there is a series of important faults with such a formula. (1) It assumes that measurement of labor conditions, market by market, can be carried on reliably, and that the data so obtained can be adjusted to compensate for differences in the relative supply of or demand for labor that are the consequence of total employment in the nation being above or below the selected policy optimum. (2) It assumes that a past labor surplus (shortage) is indicative of the future. (3) It assumes that, expressed in percentage terms, the average level of employment appropriate for the nation is a desirable goal for each individual labor market as well. (4) It assumes that comparatively modest wage adjustments will prompt adequate mobility. (5) It assumes that failure to give an absolute decrease in any market will not affect patterns of employment too adversely and that the resulting upward bias to the wage level would not be too troublesome. (6) It assumes that the proper market by market adjustment of employment levels can be accomplished within a reasonable time period through application of an identical adjustment formula in each case. (7) Under one set of circumstances, zero net gain in output per worker for the nation, it might not allow for any adjustment in relative wage rates at all. (8) Should the unlikely case of a trend decrease in national "productivity" occur, strict application of the formula would call for the reverse of appropriate wage changes.

If this simple formula for relative wage rate adjustment described above is applied without amendment, undoubtedly it will do serious harm. The above listed faults would combine to cause intense difficulties. However, some of the problems could be remedied by a change in the regulatory formula. Protection against faults four, five, seven, eight, even the approach of fault seven, could be achieved through specification of some standard other than the average of wage increases. Relaxation of the requirement that under no circumstances can absolute wages fall would give further protection. There is no compelling reason why the magnitude of adjustment to correct a surplus or shortage of labor in a particular market should be related to average wage changes for the nation. The potential disadvantages of an injunction against absolute wage decreases are significant. A formula for relative wage changes which is based upon experience and which is symmetrical in its application would be much wiser, although union objections probably would be engendered.

Problems one, two, three, and six, however, are more difficult to solve. The logical answer seems to be a more flexible wage policy. This implies the application of judgment in individual market situations. But if judgment is used in formulation of the appropriate employment goal for each market, if judgment is used to forecast future trends in particular areas, and if judgment based on relative labor supply and demand elasticities is used to determine the magnitude of the wage change in a given situation, what criteria are to be applied?

Again it becomes evident that satisfactory objective criteria for relative wage rate adjustment are not obtainable. Even the presence of accurate data, market by market, on relative levels of employment will not be sufficient information upon which to base wage adjustments.[11] Substantial administrative judgment is inevitable.

Adjustment of the Wage Package. Adjustment of the wage package is another difficult problem which a wages authority must face. Ordinarily labor-management disputes involve many issues in addition to the question of rates of pay. Sometimes these issues affect working conditions, sometimes so-called fringe benefits.

These ancillary aspects of the wage agreement affect total cost of production. Wage changes also affect cost of production. From the standpoint of management or of labor, wage changes, fringe benefits and/or improved working conditions are partial substitutes for each other. Because of this the dollar value of a change in the wage package is an additional complicating factor which must be considered by the wages authority. Adjustment of the wage package to meet needs and desires of employers and employees is important. But it also provides an avenue by which the true intent of the authority may be thwarted, as a hidden wage increase may come in the form of a fringe benefit. This is something the regulatory authority would need to guard against. It is another instance of a factor which greatly complicates the data collection and data evaluation task.

Basis of Wage Payment. Related to the issue of fringe benefits is whether the wage is to be a time wage or an efficiency wage. Intra-market comparisons will be complicated where some sectors of the market pay on one basis and others on another.

Should an efficiency wage be used as the standard throughout a given market, comparisons still might be complicated by reason of differing definitions of output. To take but three examples: (1) In the computation of output, what quality standards should be applied to determine rejected work? (2) Should any notice be taken of whether a given employee has all the work he can handle?

11. A large part of the once lengthy dispute as to the presence or absence of a shortage of engineers was partly the result of these problems. For example, has the shortage been consistent as the Engineering Manpower Commission tends to argue, or was the pre-sputnik upsurge in demand for engineers in the early 1950's a minor cross current in a context of a general surplus as Stigler and Blank contended? See, for example, David M. Blank and George J. Stigler, *The Demand and Supply of Scientific Personnel* (New York: National Bureau of Economic Research, 1957), p. 28. Or was this cross current to some extent a developing trend, as later data and W. Lee Hansen, "The 'Shortage' of Engineers," *The Review of Economics and Statistics*, August, 1961, pp. 251-256, would seem to argue.

(3) Would job descriptions be sufficiently uniform to enable comparison?

The Problem of Enforcement. A third problem worthy of attention is that of how to encourage adherence to the suggestions of the wage authority. Abba Lerner for one believes in reliance upon moral suasion,[12] with auxiliary dependence upon making inappropriate wage payments non-deductible business expense for Federal Income Tax purposes.[13] It is Lerner's contention that if wages are too high or too low in a given sector, publication of this fact would be sufficient to bring about a satisfactory adjustment. There are, however, strong reasons for doubting both the belief that moral suasion is a desirable means of enforcement and the belief that the problem of enforcement is not too severe.

Moral restraint is objectionable because it is not completely effective and because its effects are uneven. For moral restraint to be effective, offenders must be conspicuous and comparatively few in number. Preferably, also, moral restraint should reinforce other economic motives already present. These conditions are not likely to be present in the United States.

Even where moral restraint accomplishes its overall goal, inflation control in this case, it still will be inequitable. Some persons will not adhere to the "requests." Thus, moral suasion is unfair because those who exercise restraint will lose relative to those who do not. It might be added further that sometimes in the past there has been governmental coercion behind the moral restraint issue. Here the impact of the "moral restraint" would depend upon which groups the government was able to coerce.[14]

---

12. *Economics of Employment*, p. 236.

13. *Ibid.*, p. 239. At the present time it seems likely that the Federal government will attempt to strengthen U. S. guideposts by this means of fostering greater compliance. If such an approach is to be employed it is obvious that greater attention must be paid to the problems raised in Chapters 9 and 10 than heretofore. So long as the U. S. wage guideposts were at least partly just recommended policy the matter of hidden wage changes, bias in the data on surplus and shortage, etc., were not so great a problem. But once stronger measures are employed to insure compliance, greater attention needs to be devoted to the structure of the guideposts. If this is not done the investigation and enforcement aspects of guidepost policy will become needlessly complicated. This is a serious danger, for as this work has attempted to demonstrate, problems of administration would be large under the best of circumstances.

14. An example of this is President Kennedy's invocation for "guideposts for noninflationary wage and price behavior" with some success in steel and a

Several European countries, Sweden is an example, have placed heavy reliance upon moral suasion as an enforcement technique in the control of inflation. It has worked for them. However, the only countries which have employed this procedure with any real success have been relatively open economies. The people of these countries are very much aware of the need for preservation of the ability to compete in international markets. Given pegged exchange rates, this means some approximation of the general goal of price-level stability or at least a rate of inflation no more extreme than that of other trading nations. Further, in these relatively open economies, individual firms are more likely to have a vested pecuniary interest in price stability, either because they sell a product in the international market, or because they sell a component part to someone who deals in the international sphere. These general conditions are not present, to an adequate degree, in the United States.

Again the prevailing situation under present administration of the President's guideposts to non-inflationary wage bargaining serves as a useful illustration.

The government's ability to cope with guidepost violation has varied widely depending upon the particular instance, and too often securing compliance has seriously compromised other government programs and/or objectives. U. S. guidepost enforcement has been undesirable in pattern and overall impact.

For example, threat of anti trust suit has been used several times by the government to secure guidepost compliance. But, if by this kind of a trade the government secures guidepost compliance, or even worse, only the outward appearance of guidepost compliance, think of the inevitable consequences on the structure of industry. Or again, to take another example, consider the military procurement implications of shifting government purchases to favor the firm that appears to be most closely adhering to the guideposts. Or still again, consider the resources allocation problems that arise when a situation is established where some industries are forced to comply with U. S. guidepost rules because they are somehow at the mercy of the government, while other sectors of the economy go free because they are beyond the reach of the government's "peaceful" powers of persuasion.

---

few other instances, combined with a failure to achieve similar successes in other areas, *e.g.*, longshoring and construction trades.

The problem of enforcement of the wage control program is acute, and the present so-called moral suasion is not the answer.[15] The enforcement task is almost unbelievably comprehensive and criteria for judging the degree of compliance are poor. It is not sufficient to make the suggestions of a wages authority legally binding. Detailed enforcement activity also would be required if serious compromise with wage pattern and/or wage level objectives is to be avoided. It is doubtful if a national incomes policy program of the surplus-shortage type could succeed even partially if enforcement was as lax as, for example, it is under the Fair Labor Standards Act or as it is under the present wage guideposts. More than this, the motives for voluntary compliance also would need to be strong, as, for example, they were during wartime. Otherwise the likelihood of a macro-economic bias towards an inflationary wage bill will have to be accepted. As with any law or government program, any national incomes policy would need at least the passive support of most of the people most of the time.[16]

15. What recently has passed for moral suasion frequently has gone beyond any reasonable definition of the term anyway. To illustrate, in the 1962 labor dispute involving the Gulf and Atlantic Coast longshoring industry over work rules and pay, D. A. Wren, in an unpublished doctoral dissertation, identified eight separate government actions that were designed to bring major pressure to bear in favor of a settlement that would fall within the 3.2 general guidepost rule. These measures included a Taft-Hartley injunction, personal intervention by the Secretary of Labor, a Senate investigating committee, simultaneous use of over 100 professional mediators from the Federal Mediation and Conciliation Service, and threat of punative Federal legislation that would make future longshoring disputes subject to compulsory arbitration. "Governmental Intervention in Labor-Management Disputes, 1961-1963" (School of Business, University of Illinois, 1964). George L. Perry, "Wages and the Guideposts," *American Economic Review*, September, 1967, pp. 897-904, uses data on wage movements in two-digit manufacturing industries to demonstrate, by a study of over-all wage pattern changes, what Wren demonstrated by example. What Perry does is separately to determine which industries are visible in the sense that they are highly susceptible to guidepost enforcement pressures, and which are invisible. Perry then shows that, while the guideposts probably have had a general anti-inflation effect, this result seemingly has been accompanied by a distortion of wage patterns and relative prices.

16. It might be thought that only under a Nazi-Soviet type system would this form of what amounts to compulsory arbitration be successful. In other cases disapproving parties, unions or management, could be so uncooperative as to render any wage decision inoperative. Actually, this does not state the issue strongly enough. Even under a Nazi-Soviet system wage regulation must be reasonable or it is likely to be unworkable. Soviet experiences in the 1930's appear to illustrate this latter point rather well. Franklyn D. Holzman, "Soviet Inflationary Pressures, 1928-1957: Causes and Cures," *Quarterly Journal of Economics*, May, 1960, pp. 167-88, argues there is considerable evidence to

A variety of enforcement powers could be made available to whatever administrative body ultimately was charged with the task of implementing the controls. But it would be difficult to determine the extent of adherence to rulings of the selected wages authority. The same methods by which the regulated areas might bias the raw data available to the wages authority could be used to hide lack of compliance from the authority. Indeed such a practice seems inevitable, and inevitably it would be difficult if not impossible to uncover.

CONCLUSION

Investigation of administrative aspects of a detailed national incomes policy program indicates a host of problems arising from inability to determine a set of regulatory criteria that are both administratively workable and economically satisfactory. Economically correct criteria for wage adjustment exist, but, under many circumstances, problems of implementation seem so difficult as to vitiate the program as a useful policy tool. Certainly investigation indicates that the task of wages administration can be expected to be costly, haphazard, cumbersome, and somewhat arbitrary.

---

indicate that inflation experienced in the Soviet Union during the 1930's was wage inflation in origin. This in spite of the fact that wages were set by law. Employment and output objectives apparently were much too ambitious. Input factors were relatively fixed, with the exception of labor which was free to move. As a result workers moved from job to job as managers raided each other for workers. In response to secret wage concessions (upgrading of workers' skills, unofficial bonuses, etc.) worker mobility ran as high as an average of one and one-half times per year for major firms. Moreover the problems described seem to be continuing ones. Robert Fearn in his review of the U.S.S.R.'s problems in 1961 and 1962 ("Controls Over Wage Trends and Inflationary Pressures in the U.S.S.R.," *Industrial and Labor Relations Review*, January, 1965, pp. 186-95) finds much the same sort of thing existing currently.

Chapter 11

NATIONAL INCOMES POLICY IN WAGE
INFLATION SITUATIONS

Part II has been devoted to the central question posed: can national incomes policy, properly structured, be an effective complement to monetary and fiscal arrangements for control of wage inflation?

The analysis specifically has depended upon the assumption that past inflationary experiences often have resulted from excessive money wage increases and from downward wage rigidities. The supposition is that these forces, which combine to yield an upward bias in wage rates, always have been present. They may not have been visible when excess aggregate monetary demand resulted in greater inflation than the wage-push forces would have caused, but the upward wage pressures still have been present. It is within this framework, then, that wage controls have been examined.

If it is a question of non wage-push situations and non stabilization objectives, investigation reveals a variety of types of wage controls used in the past or suggested for use. Wage controls may place a ceiling on wages or a floor under wages. Again wage controls may be partial or general; they may be flexible or inflexible. Wage control policies may concentrate on the regulation of relative wage rates, or they may involve regulation of relative wage rates only insofar as this is necessary to control the aggregate wage bill. Finally, administration of the controls may be very thoroughgoing or it may be somewhat sporadic.

However, this wide choice of control measures is not available to the policy maker concerned with control of wage inflation, without attendant adverse employment and price-level consequences. The wage control program selected must have a number of specific properties. It must be all-pervasive. It must be long-lasting. It must fit well into the macro-economic environment. It must be flexible enough to permit appropriate resource allocation. And it must be economical to administer. This rules out most wage control techniques.

There are not many wage control criteria which could be adapted to fit the macro-economic environment, given wage inflation. Here the objective must be the highest national wage level compatible with full employment-full capacity levels of production. This requires that the regulation program selected be reasonably able to control the general wage level. This is important for, given the existence of wage inflation, the macro targets selected will not be achievable unless governmental involvement in the wage setting process has the net result of successfully holding down the rate of increase in the general level of wages without promoting distortion in wage patterns more serious than the inflation which is the alternative. In the absence of the incomes policy there would be a tendency for wages to be too high. This must be prevented.

The above implies need both to measure the wage level appropriate, and to measure the wage level that would result from a specified administrative action. It also implies that the national wage level should not fluctuate greatly over short time periods.

Chapter 7 makes the point that any of four general principles of adjustment might be used as a guide to the aggregate wage appropriate. These are: adjustment according to supply and demand, relative shares as an adjustment criterion, adjustment according to measured changes in output per worker, and adjustment in response to political or social pressures.

Adjustment according to supply and demand is the theoretically most appropriate criterion. It also would be the most difficult of the four to administer because of the intense problems of definition and of measurement which it evokes. Adjustment so as to maintain relative income shares, while not based upon quite so firm a theoretical base as adjustment according to supply and demand, does have much in its favor as it seems to reflect the way in which the economy has behaved in the past. The problems in its implementation, while not so severe as for adjustment according to supply and demand, again are those of definition and measurement.

Adjustment according to measured changes in output per worker would be more capable of administration than either adjustment according to supply and demand or adjustment according to relative income share data. Adjustment according to measured changes in output per worker, in principle, would work much the same as adjustment according to relative share data and would have much the same arguments in its favor. The primary difference between the two is that adjustment according to relative share data develops a wage level guide on the basis of shifts in the wage bill, while adjustment according to output per worker deals with wage level adjustments solely. Adjustment according to social and/or political pressures is the least objective and least appropriate, from a theoretical utopian standpoint, of the four criteria suggested. Presumably, the argument for use of this criterion would be political expediency.

In spite of individual differences, if proponents of the wage inflation thesis are correct in assuming that the unregulated economy tends toward a disappointingly low level of employment, then given price stabilizing monetary and fiscal policy, initially all four adjustment formulae would function with some success. But they would be likely to function less and less well the longer they were in force. The greatest weakness of available macro-economic criteria for wage adjustment is that they are not long-lasting. Each would have a tendency to cumulative error. This would be particularly true of adjustment according to relative income shares and adjustment according to productivity change as these measures require the application of rather rigid formulas which are based upon past experience and are not perfect reflections of what has happened in the past, and, therefore, are unlikely to be exact predictors of what should happen in the future. But the remark that the macro-economic criteria used would have a tendency to cumulate error also is true of the other two measures, adjustment according to supply and demand and adjustment according to social and/or political pressures. Both these measures hinge upon definitions which are based upon past experience.

Since no objective criterion for macro-economic wage adjustment exists which is at one and the same time theoretically correct and administratively feasible in the sense of being perfectly objective, experience under conditions of an unregulated market must be relied upon to some degree. The more the economy recedes from such a situation, the less relevant is this experience as a policy guide.

By contrast with the macro case, there is only one guide to the adjustment of relative wages that offers any real chance for success. This is to relate adjustments in relative wage rates to the degree of unemployment, market by market. This is, of course, a micro-economic guide which enjoys a number of similarities with the possible macro-economic guide of adjustment according to supply and demand. This similarity was discussed in Chapter 8.

Other criteria for micro-economic wage adjustment, ability to pay, minimum budgets, wage comparisons, or output per worker statistics, do not permit development of an appropriate wage pattern. They fail in this respect either because they are not sufficiently flexible or because they are not properly flexible. The former failing is suggested by the wage comparison and minimum budget criteria, the latter by the guides of ability to pay and productivity. These criteria are theoretically inappropriate because the wages to which they lead fail to approximate the defined optimum (where marginal revenue product and average cost of labor acquisition schedules intersect) at least as well as the unregulated market.

The guide to adjustment of relative wage rates that is selected must foster the development of an appropriate wage structure. This includes development of a pattern of wages at least as good as that found in the absence of governmental involvement in the wage setting process and the avoidance of an upward bias in the macro-economic wage. Failures in both areas are very real possibilities to which past control programs often have succumbed. They result from failure properly to offset wage increases with comparative decreases, from failure to achieve adequate control over all wage movements, and from application of an adjustment principle which does not pay proper attention to shifting conditions in individual labor markets.

Under the right circumstances a national incomes policy program based on market by market unemployment could meet a number of the requirements of a good criterion for relative wage rate adjustment. It could be sufficiently all-pervasive. It could be economical to administer. It could be quite flexible. The difficulty is that it would not be properly flexible in all circumstances. The real question thus becomes: What are these circumstances and are they likely to occur?

The above does not mean, of course, that such a program ever would achieve theoretical perfection. Two aspects of the adjustment formulae combine to prevent this, regardless of the circumstances of application. (1) Guides to an "optimum" macro-economic wage are imperfect. (2) The selected micro-economic welfare optimum of setting the wage where the marginal revenue product and average cost of labor acquisition schedules intersect is open to some criticism, particularly if the selected unemployment target for each labor market (expressed in percentage terms) is the same as the unemployment target for the nation.

These are unavoidable problems. But they need not be vitiating. The world is imperfect now. Not only are many individual markets structured in such a way as to impart a wage bias in one direction or another, but the wage inflation thesis suggests a general bias upward in all money wages. Final judgment as to whether national incomes policy would introduce more faults than it would cure is much more likely to hinge upon the practical problem of implementing the adjustment formulae and upon intensity of need for the policy, than upon whether, under any circumstances, the formulae used could hope to reach theoretical perfection.

The more significant problems of implementation surround the issue of data collection and data evaluation. In a sense the national incomes policy outlined is extremely permissive. In order to avoid excessive administrative expense and to enable the greatest possible regard for individual market preferences, it tries to place heavy reliance upon information supplied by individual workers (or their representatives) and employers, particularly the latter. Under the wage criterion given, aid from these groups is depended upon to furnish raw data relevant to the task for determining the supply of, relative to the demand for, labor in each individual labor market.

Thus problems are likely to arise whenever there is economic incentive to achieve a wage other than one which would have been set by an administrator in full possession of all known facts;

that is, where labor markets are imperfectly competitive or where the macro-economic target is such that all labor markets have an economic incentive to bias wage data.

Of course, the mere presence of economic incentive to bias the wage does not guarantee that bias will occur. In the first place, monopoly and monopsony power exists in labor markets now that is not exploited in a manner detrimental to economic efficiency. Quite frequently employers, when faced with a rising supply curve of labor, do not appear to take advantage of the situation to force down the rate of employment and hence the level of wages. Similarly, union monopolists often do not seem to exploit their position by cutting employment so as to force wages up. In the second place, even where monopoly or monopsony power now exists and is exploited in a manner detrimental to economic efficiency, this does not guarantee that the practice will continue after a national incomes policy is imposed. Workers and employers just might consent, without conniving or subterfuge, to abide by the adjustment formulae deemed desirable.

But both the above points beg a portion of the question. The relevant issue is not whether some markets would cooperate fully with a national incomes policy program, given economic incentive to bias the data, but whether all or most of them will. For the United States the greater possibility is that, given economic incentive, many or most markets will bias the data. There are, then, many similarities between these situations and the earlier discussion concerning the efficacy of moral suasion as a policy possibility. Some groups will adhere in letter and spirit to the regulations; others will not. Thus, where incentive to bias the results does not exist, both the raw data supplied to government investigators and the degree of compliance with administrative directives and suggestions will be suspect.

Unfortunately, the program outlined does not enable an outsider to ascertain the true facts in instances of this kind. Moreover, many of these problems of verification seem insurmountable. This would hold true even if, to the best of human ability, the ends and means of the incomes policy were reproduced faithfully by an enforcement agency. A part of the problem is one of objective standards by which to judge the issues. At least an equal portion, however, is one of the costliness of the extensive, formal investigation necessary for verification of suspect data.

From this it might be assumed falsely that a national incomes policy program which relies upon private sources to furnish the raw data upon which wage adjustment recommendations would be based: (1) would be most disruptive where it was employed to combat the type of inflation for which the policy might seem best suited—price inflation caused by excessive wage increases, because here pressures for general wage increases would be translated into incentive to bias labor market data; and (2) least disruptive where it was employed to combat the type of inflation for which the policy might seem least suited—price inflation with a cause other than excessive wage increases, because here no pressures for general wage increases would exist. In other words, a national incomes policy guide administered in anti wage inflation ways either would be inappropriate or superfluous. In wage inflation situations it would be inappropriate.[1] But this misleads. There are two avenues which an incomes policy might take, depending upon the type of wage inflation existing, that would represent possible means by which this apparent conundrum might be avoided. The first is not to depend upon those who would seek to impart an upward bias to wages for wage data. The second is not to apply the policy with equal vigor in all markets.

Chapter 9 demonstrated that there are a number of natural advantages to relying quite heavily upon employer supplied data, rather than upon worker or union supplied data, for most of the basic information necessary to wage rate adjustment. It is this reality of the wage administration task which provides the first important avenue by which to avoid the dilemma that in application national incomes policy formulae are apt to be most inadequate where general pressures to bias the wage are greatest, which is where the policy might seem to be most needed.

An inflationary experience that stems from inappropriate increases in wages could be eliminated effectively through the application of the adjustment guides adopted if several conditions were fulfilled, i.e., (1) employers were to supply the responsible wages authority with the necessary raw data. (2) Employers oppose downward wage rigidities and inflationary wage increases, and have accepted them in the past only because they were backed by coercive authority on the part of labor. (3) A national incomes

1. Wage controls in non wage inflation situations is the subject of the next chapter.

policy would eliminate labor's coercive power.[2] (4) Elimination of labor's coercive power and reliance on an employer wage would not so distort wage patterns in individual markets as to more than offset any anti-inflationary value which the policy would have.

Usual versions of the wage inflation explanation, inflation the result of excessive bargaining power of labor, and inflation the result of wage rigidities, represent situations where labor gains an inappropriate money wage level and an inappropriate wage pattern, over the objections of employers. When past inflationary experiences are attributed to excessive bargaining power of labor, the contention probably is that employers do not favor the resulting wage structure, but that somehow they are powerless to prevent it. The idea that wages are relatively inflexible downward, but relatively flexible upward, the wage rigidities explanation, also carries some implication that employers would oppose the downward rigidities if they had the power to do so.

If labor has the power to set an inflationary wage, which employers oppose and would not accept without coercion, it could be the result of monopolistic power on the part of labor. This would not always be the case. Wage rigidities may occur without labor unions even being present. Excessive bargaining power of labor also might exist without the presence of labor unions. The point that spontaneous wage increase might occur in the absence of trade unions, or without their being the active force, was developed in Chapter 3. Worker preoccupation with "money illusion" is one possible explanation; general belief in future price-level increases combined with a desire to anticipate and offset them through wage increases is another. And, if upward wage pressures were prevalent, but not the result of union activity, an employer wage would not seem to offer any special advantages. However, some past inflationary experiences may be traced to union monopoly activity.

The possibility that union monopolies represent an inflationary force which a national incomes policy program might neutralize thus represents an important exception to the provisional statement that national supervision of private wage adjustments would be

---

2. As pointed out in Chapter 9, the mere fact that wages are imposed under the authority of the central government would not guarantee full compliance with the letter and spirit of regulations. In this case, if labor will not cooperate with a given wage, employers are likely not to suggest it, through the data they supply to public administrators.

most effective in establishing an appropriate pattern of wages where it was least needed. However, it raises another provocative issue, not central to this work, but still intriguing. If union monopolies are to blame for certain inflationary experiences, why select the somewhat devious route of a national incomes policy as a means of limiting this monopoly power? Why not take a more direct approach and prohibit unions altogether? Alternatively why not prohibit union participation in wage setting activities including fringe benefit issues?

Those who advocate some sort of incomes policy as an anti-inflationary device ordinarily do not deal with these questions, at least not directly. And, as previously indicated, wage-push theorists may not even consider unions to blame for inability of the economy to obtain and maintain high employment. But one possible answer to the questions posed would be that unions perform many functions outside or beyond participation in wage determination and related issues. These other functions are important and should be preserved, and they best can be preserved by the introduction of an incomes policy.

Specifically, to give but three frequently cited advantages, it might be argued that American trade unions: (1) help the worker achieve status in the work-place through such procedures as careful prescription of work rules and close adherence to a formalized procedure for handling labor-management disagreements, (2) provide workers with a social organization, (3) represent a means by which workers can be bound into a cohesive force, and thus facilitate the bargaining process in some instances as management then can deal with a representative individual rather than with the workers one at a time.

However, while the subsidiary "benefits" of unionization may be recognized, it should be understood that it is not possible to eliminate a union's wage setting authority and leave these other activities unaffected. With an effective incomes policy aimed at preventing union "excesses," presumably there should come denial of the right to strike for higher wages, for fringe benefits, for changed work rules, or for anything else concerning terms and conditions of employment which measurably would affect the supply of labor, the demand for labor, or the effective time or efficiency wage. Without limitations on the right to strike, a governmental wage control program seems doomed. It would lack the requisite ability to encourage even minimal compliance with its edicts. Yet with such a prohibition the effectiveness of any union is imperiled.[3]

The right to strike in order to influence terms and conditions of employment is a cornerstone upon which successful union activity has been developed and maintained in this country. Without these strike powers a union would not be able to exert coercion to influence intra-plant policies by the employer. Thus, under an incomes policy program of the type outlined, those functions of American trade unions now second in importance to wage setting activities, participation in the determination of fringe benefits, working conditions and work rules would also be impaired drastically.

It is true that imposition of a national incomes policy program could mean new duties for the typical union. Unions might be expected to act as labor's representative before some sort of national wages committee. But on balance the net effect of such a policy would be the end of trade unionism as it is known in this country, perhaps even the end of the American trade union movement itself. This latter development is not inevitable, but it seems not unlikely. The alternate possibility is that a new brand of unionism might emerge, as it has in other countries where a national incomes policy has been established, and in this country temporarily when wage controls were in force during periods of national emergency, where primary emphasis is placed on such things as national political activities and general social reform.

The precise response to an incomes policy of American unions and of American union membership is uncertain. But if unions respond with development of political power this might enable them to thwart the objectives of the program through activity in the political arena. Should this eventuality become reality, effective implementation of an incomes policy obviously would require abolition of union political activity of this sort as well as sharp re-

---

3. Perhaps for this reason unionized workers often strike even where such actions are prohibited by law. The rash of strikes in this country by affected state and local government employees is illustrative of the point. Recent Australian experience under compulsory arbitration is another example of this point. The number of Australian workers that go on strike annually has amounted to some 66 out of every 1,000 which is a strike incidence about double that of the United States and even more than that for many other countries. It is four times the rate for Sweden, for example, and nearly three times the rate for the United Kingdom.

strictions on union bargaining at both the firm and industry levels.

The possibility that, given a national incomes policy program, American trade unions would respond with a change in their tactics, indeed in their general approach, is an obvious one. The possibility that this development would take the form of increased political activity seems quite likely. The degree to which trade unions involve themselves in wage decisions in those free world nations that do have some sort of national incomes policy certainly points strongly in this direction.

Should trade unions succeed in making the subject of wage policy decisions a political issue it seems uncertain that the nation's incomes policy program would be administered solely in anti wage-push ways. The especial dangers are that the general wage level would be too high, that favored political groups would receive favored wage consideration, and that too strong an egalitarian trend in wage rates might prevail.

The second avenue of approach by which the administrative task of a national incomes policy program might be minimized is that of partial controls. Partial controls might be used in conjunction with a plan to rely primarily upon employer information for basic wage data, or partial controls might be used in lieu of such a plan. Partial controls might be partial only in the sense that the incomes policy was not actively administered in all sectors, or the scope of the controls might be limited by law or by formal administrative procedures.

Reliance upon employers for basic wage data, which is tantamount, really, to having an employer wage, has the advantage of greatly facilitating the wage administration process. But this advantage is gained at the expense of removing any barriers to a monopsony wage. Further, success of the approach hinges upon the assumption that employers oppose wage rigidities and inflationary wage increases, that employers have yielded to these pressures in the past only because of coercive authority on the part of labor, and that, should employers be those who supplied necessary wage data to the responsible governmental authority, this coercive power effectively would be neutralized.

Reliance upon partial controls represents a means by which some of the disadvantages of an employer wage might be reduced or eliminated. Where used in conjunction with reliance primarily upon employer supplied wage data, partial controls could allow labor markets to operate freely, and presumably more effectively, in all areas except those likely to generate inflationary pressures. Where used in lieu of heavy reliance upon employer data as a guide to relative wage rate adjustments, partial controls suggest the need for intense administrative effort and considerable skill in judgment. But placing limits on the areas which would require attention reduces the scope of the administrative task and facilitates the administration process as it enables comparisons between these sectors and others that presumably do not need attention.

Not every form of wage inflation suggests, as feasible, partial controls. Wage inflation, the result of general wage pressures throughout the economy, clearly does not suggest such an approach. Moreover, the mere fact that wage inflation originally was the fault of wage increases in a small sector of the labor market does not constitute a prima facie case in support of partial controls. It is necessary to know if a general wage inflation response is so conditioned that it would continue even if the initial stimulus were removed.

Two aspects of wage inflation theory suggest the wisdom of partial controls, but each suggests partial controls of a somewhat different nature. If, by wage inflation, what is meant is union wage inflation, the idea of controls on unions alone is an obvious thought. If partial controls were used in this case, as a practical matter it might be wisest to have the procedure somewhat informal. The political advantages of not calling undue attention to an "anti union bias" in the controls would seem significant even to a political non-initiate. If, as a cause of inflation, heavy emphasis is placed upon the role of downward wage rigidities, partial controls again are a possibility. In this case, however, the sectors covered would be those experiencing a relative, or absolute, decline in labor demand. This would be a shifting group. The existence of downward wage rigidities calls for partial controls, but partial controls on different sectors of the labor market at different times.

A final possible way in which partial controls might be used is as a means of combatting key wage inflations. Not many economists propound the idea that an identifiable market, like that for steel or auto manufacture, might be guilty of stimulating an inflationary round. It is a generally accepted thesis that the inflationary process is sequential rather than simultaneous, but it is not generally accepted that any one sector is the inevitable initiator. Prices and wages, it is agreed, are adjusted in some markets and

the effects of these plus other changes then spread widely throughout the economy. But of course this type of inflation theory is
much different from the version of round inflation theory that
selects a small area or sector of the economy as uniquely culpable.

Given the unique starters version of round inflation, the incomes policy program outlined, with the partial control feature,
ought to be as adaptable to this situation as to any that might be
considered. But if, as most economists believe, the starters of an
inflationary process are not unique, and if increases in, say, auto and
steel are prevented the inflationary process then would just begin
somewhere else, construction and metal fabricating for example,
then the partial control idea will be of no value and wage controls will be effective only to the extent that general wage controls
are useful in combating general wage-push inflation.

The most logical candidate for national incomes policy as an
anti-inflationary device is wage inflation. However, when the proposal of wage adjustment to control wage inflation is considered,
it is not possible to generalize and say that the impact of a national
incomes policy would be this or that. Given wage inflation, the
impact of a national incomes policy as an inflation deterrent would
depend in part upon the specific policy program instituted, in part
upon the strength of the upward wage pressures, and in part upon
the cause of the wage pressures.

Wage inflation may be the result of excessive wage demands
on the part of the workers in general, or on the part of unionized
workers only, or on the part of just a section or segment of the work
force.

In other words a problem of scope is raised at this point. If
wage inflation refers to an upward bias in prices coming from excessive wage demands of both wage earners and salaried personnel,
then, to be most effective, the wage control program must encom-
pass both groups. If the responsibility for price inflation could be
placed on only one of these groups then the controls might be
placed on that group only. Of course this latter statement would
apply only so long as the original hypothesis (that, for example,
wage earners were the only ones to blame) remained valid. Thus,
for example, if wage controls resulted in wage earners migrating
to self employment or to salaried occupations and if, after moving
into the new situation, they represented a cost-push force, then
available control measures would need to be broadened to encom-

pass this development. Otherwise the measures would lose force.

Upward wage pressures which are the result of union monopoly power might be contained effectively by administrative involvement in the wage setting process, if the responsible authority relied primarily upon employer supplied wage data. Such a program could be directed towards all workers or just those unionized. If the program encompassed all workers this would mean that restrictions would be imposed on some "blameless" workers. To avoid this criticism the program might be directed against unionized workers only. The latter would seem a more appropriately tailored program. In either case a national incomes policy program offers some promise of success. The final issue hinges upon the relative merits of inflation elimination versus those of allowing employers to set a possibly monopsonistic wage.

To the extent that wage inflation pressures would exist even without trade union interference, a national incomes policy would be useful only if employees and employers could be induced towards reasonable compliance with the principles underlying the policy. But as already has been explained, this is precisely the kind of situation where compliance is least likely to be adequate. This is where incentive to bias the raw data is strongest. Here, judgment would have to be applied by the wages authority, based upon investigation of the facts of the situation. Chapters 9 and 10 both indicated that great difficulties would have to be overcome if an incomes policy were to perform satisfactorily under these conditions. If those difficulties were not overcome, the pattern and quite likely the level of wages would not be at all appropriate, and it would be hard to justify the policy.

If, instead of union wage pressures or general wage pressures, upward wage pressures in just a sector of the economy were responsible for starting an inflationary round, partial controls again would be a possibility. Control or pressure might be directed only against those wages that were regarded as the "starters." As an example, if steel and auto wages were considered to be the culprits, sanctions might be placed on these two areas. Of course, as in the case of union induced wage inflation, general adjustment formulae might be applied in all instances even though general application would not be needed. But again, this would subject many "blameless" groups to the indignities of outside supervision. It also would complicate the administrative task greatly.

Obviously, given wage inflation, the desirability of some sort of national incomes policy as an anti-inflationary device hinges upon the disadvantages of an incomes policy relative to the disadvantages of that combination of unemployment and inflation which is presumed to be the alternative. But the comparison is a difficult one and depends upon such factors as: are the upward wage pressures the results of union monopoly activity or not, how closely will any administrative authority conform to proper principles for wage administration, and is the current balance of payments situation such as to make the impact of inflation unusually severe.[4]

However, the alternative of an actively administered national incomes policy offers a number of special disadvantages which would not be associated with wage inflation. Such an incomes policy would be expensive to administer. The more thoroughgoing the administrative procedures the more expensive they would be. Inflation, on the other hand, is not the result of a detailed and expensive government program. Macro-economic formulae for wage regulation are imperfect and likely to become more so the longer they are in force. Formulae for calculation of the magnitude of the wage change appropriate in a given market situation are either inadequate or depend upon a great deal of administrative judgment and experimentation. Moreover, these same remarks apply equally to selection of market by market employment goals. Also, of course, a detailed national incomes policy program, if applied with any real force, would interfere with certain existing functions of American trade unionism, while the presence of inflation is likely to facilitate these functions. This, too, is an effect many would consider a disadvantage.

In addition to these definite disadvantages, some of the effects of a policy such as that outlined are uncertain. The practical value of the technique of successive approximation in the wage setting process is not clear. Attempts to make frequent corrections in wage patterns might do more harm than good. The relationship which an incomes policy program would have with price stabilizing

4. This approach depends upon the assumption that balance of payments problems intensify the need for inflation control, but do not necessarily make inflation control mandatory. The political and economic consequences of devaluation, for example, might be preferable to the misallocation of resources associated with a national incomes policy for inflation control. It would depend upon the wage control procedures that could be implemented and the over-all seriousness of the balance of payments situation.

monetary and fiscal arrangements also is uncertain. Conceivably, an incomes policy would facilitate monetary and fiscal arrangements aimed at price level stabilization. Or they might hinder such an activity.

Because of the clear and obvious disadvantages of a national incomes policy program that is at all effectively administered, and because of the uncertainty about some of its effects, caution should be employed when deciding upon its use. In other words, the policy should be introduced only when it promises substantial improvement over the existing situation, not simply when it offers a chance of success. Given wage inflation, the policy would appear to meet this test when a central or outside wage authority could place heavy reliance upon the information supplied to it, because the source of information was both privy to the necessary facts and not biased towards maintenance either of wage rigidities or a "too high" wage rate moving upward "too quickly," or when the scope of the controls need not be large. These are conditions that might be fulfilled. Even under the assumption of wage inflation, it is by no means certain that they would be fulfilled.

PART III

Non Wage Inflation Situations

Chapter 12

NATIONAL INCOMES POLICY IN NON WAGE INFLATION SITUATIONS

Part II analyzed the efficacy of national incomes policy as an adjunct to monetary and fiscal policy for control of wage inflation. At that time no effort was made to evaluate a national incomes policy program used in anti wage inflation ways, but applied to non wage-push inflation. This chapter is designed to rectify that omission. Specifically, the purpose is to indicate, in general, the ways in which conclusions reached in Part II would need to be adjusted when inflationary pressures were not of the wage-push type.

It is not the intent to engage in a detailed and exhaustive analysis of the use of an incomes policy in these other situations. The central question posed by this work is: Can national incomes policy be an effective aid to control of wage inflation, the result either of excessive money wage increases or of downward rigidities in money wages? This chapter is designed only to survey a closely related question: If the above described wage-push theory of inflation is not valid, can such a national incomes policy program ease the task of price stabilizing monetary and fiscal policy; and if so, at what cost?

To accomplish this objective, each of the theories of inflation discussed in Chapter 3, with the exception of the wage inflation explanation, will be examined in turn. As in that chapter, the analysis will commence with the demand-pull explanation. It then will move

163

to consideration of the several rebuttals to the demand-pull hypothesis.

NATIONAL INCOMES POLICY AND DEMAND INFLATION

The usual view is that demand inflation ought to be controlled through monetary and fiscal policy. Under these conditions, a national incomes policy typically would be thought to be redundant.[1] Demand inflation results from excessive increases in aggregate demand. The orthodox means of neutralizing these increases is monetary and fiscal policy.

Certainly monetary and fiscal policy could be sufficient for demand inflation control. This would be so if policy could be designed effectively to stabilize the level of aggregate monetary demand so as to obtain and maintain reasonable price stability. The usual assumption is that if this were possible, an incomes policy would not be necessary for inflation control with continued high levels of employment. Under these same circumstances, an incomes policy would be detrimental insofar as the impact was an altered pattern of resource allocation, brought about as the result either of a level or pattern of wages that was inappropriate.

In other words, the structure and level of wages affect cost of production and, therefore, aggregate supply. If the dual goal of full employment-full capacity levels of output plus price-level stability is to be served, the wage pattern and wage level must be economically correct. Given demand-pull inflation and adequate monetary and fiscal policy, the customary assumption is that economic forces would work to bring about such a pattern and level of wages without the aid of any direct involvement by the government in private negotiation over wages. Under these same assumptions, erroneous national wage policy would have a deleterious effect, while proper wage policy could not improve upon the unregulated market.

Given price-level stability, the assumption that an incomes policy could make no contribution to economic efficiency is incorrect. The prediction is likely, but not certain. The preceding chap-

1. The argument, not universally adhered to, in favor of direct controls in time of total war is an exception to this. Here, however, the true impact of the controls would be to force a change in relative shares by means other than tax increases.

ter made the point that there are several positive disadvantages to a national incomes policy: it is likely to be costly to administer, it employs imperfect standards for wage adjustments, etc. These disadvantages cannot be overcome completely, but they could be offset if adoption of an incomes policy resulted in the elimination of some of the undesirable wage and employment effects of existing market imperfections. The eventuality is improbable, but not impossible. It would depend upon how the policy was administered.

By contrast, the assumption that monetary and fiscal policy can be designed to stabilize effectively the level of prices and that, therefore, limits to private bargaining over wages are unnecessary as a stabilization device, is open to serious criticism. Monetary and fiscal policy is not all that accurate. An incomes policy might help stabilize price-levels.

Chapter 6, particularly, endeavored to illustrate the point that price stabilizing monetary and fiscal policy would be highly inaccurate. These failings have many causes; but, behavior of the wage sector is a part of the problem. Faulty prediction of wage changes is a perennial difficulty, because of the unforeseen influence on price-level movements which these changes have. Wage changes which fail to reinforce monetary and fiscal policy objectives are another difficulty. Wage behavior is of vital importance to stabilization policy. Not only do wage changes affect price-level movements through their impact on cost of production, and therefore aggregate supply, but also through their impact on levels of income, consumption, and therefore aggregate monetary demand.

It is evident that wage policy cannot be dissociated from monetary and fiscal policy and that, properly structured, an incomes policy could assist the speed and accuracy of price stabilization policies. But, if a national incomes policy program were employed as a means of aiding price stability, given demand inflation, to be most effective it would need to be operated in other than anti wage-push ways. Two possibilities suggest themselves.

The objective of the policy could be to minimize change. To the degree that the objective was accomplished uncertainty about wage shifts would be reduced. Equally, such a policy could help minimize any complicating influence of chain reactions, the result of interdependence between wages and the level of economic activity, whereby a change in monetary and fiscal policy influences the level and structure of wages, which in turn affects price-level movements, with consequences in monetary and fiscal policy, etc.

As a second possible objective, national incomes policy could attempt to reinforce monetary and fiscal policy through supporting wage shifts. This is much the more complicated approach. It would require that the policy maker have some idea of timing, direction, and magnitude of wage changes needed to facilitate monetary and fiscal policy in any given situation, plus an ability to implement changes deemed appropriate. The procedure suggests itself only on condition that these issues could be settled with some accuracy and then only if it could be established that a significant deficiency of monetary and fiscal policy is lack of adequately powerful controls. Both of these conditions are unrealistic.

However, the two policy suggestions put forth thus far are peripheral. Regardless of their merits for stabilization policy, they have in common the unfortunate characteristic that they are aimed at facilitating price-level stabilization irrespective of output and employment consequences. This is a serious and probably vitiating defect. The attractive attribute of national incomes policy as an aid to inflation regulation is that the policy is intended to minimize labor surpluses (shortages), market by market and for the nation as a whole, so as to achieve maximum employment. It is, then, for good reason as well as expositional convenience that the important question is whether, given demand-pull inflation, a national incomes program designed primarily to combat wage-push inflation also would facilitate price-level stabilization, not whether some other policy program would do that job better, if at the same time output and employment objectives were sacrificed.

In the face of demand inflation, the supporting influence of an incomes policy administered in anti wage-push ways is not predictable. At least it is not completely predictable. There would be times when wage movements and changes in the supply of money, or of governmental budgetary balance, ought not be positively correlated. Most of the time, of course, the changes ought to be directly related. Even so, wage changes and monetary and fiscal policy changes ought not to be proportionate or a constant ratio. Wage rates and wage levels adjusted in accord with the principles set forth in Chapters 7 and 8 usually would reinforce monetary and fiscal policy. But the degree of support would vary from one situation to another. Since both of these statements also apply to the influence of unregulated wages, it is uncertain whether the incomes policy program suggested would reinforce price stabilizing monetary and fiscal policy any better or more often than unregulated wages.

Whether an incomes policy designed primarily to counter wage inflation could facilitate price stabilizing monetary and fiscal policy in another way by providing greater wage stability and predictability also is in doubt. The point was developed in Chapter 10 and elsewhere that the policy might tend to more infrequent wage change. At least this should be attempted. If so, and if successful, this would be of some help in the formulation of stabilization policies. Even more important, given this sort of wage adjustment formula, wage administrators would have access to a wealth of labor market data and, of course, would be more cognizant of the principles upon which wage changes were based. This should enable more accurate prediction of wage level changes and of wage structure changes than heretofore has been possible.

However, prediction of wage changes could be quite accurate and yet prediction of the price-level effects of the changes still might be very poor. Then too, as mentioned in Chapter 6, if wage changes are made simultaneously, or nearly so, with changes in monetary and fiscal policy this could be most disruptive. Again, the disruptive effect would flow from inability accurately to predict price-level consequences of wage changes.

It seems likely that any incomes policy applied in anti wage-push ways, given demand inflation, would cause the wage structure and wage level to be inappropriate in the sense that even slightly controlled wages would not work to promote as efficient an allocation of labor among markets or as high a level of employment as otherwise would occur. This is not because an incomes policy would work poorly. Quite the contrary, the wage authority ought to be better able to obtain compliance with its recommendations, given demand inflation, than would be the case given wage inflation. The problem is that under demand inflation the structure and level of wages would approximate the optimum about as well without an incomes policy. Thus, it is more difficult for national incomes policy to make a positive contribution here in the sense of fostering a more perfect wage structure and level.

Whether national incomes policy to combat wage inflation would facilitate stabilization policy, even if at the expense of economic efficiency, is much less certain. It would depend upon how the policy was administered. It would depend upon how well public administrators and others could learn to work with the policy.

On balance, given demand-pull inflation, it seems probable that a national incomes policy program administered in anti wage-push ways would not be unusually harmful or helpful. This conclusion is not so empty as it might seem. It contradicts a common view that incomes policy is totally inappropriate given demand inflation. It permits the judgment that national incomes policy should be imposed to combat, say wage-push inflation, even though inflation is not always of that type, but sometimes demand-pull.

NATIONAL INCOMES POLICY AND COST INFLATION

A second major category of inflation, against which national incomes policy might be considered, is cost inflation. The impact of such a policy as a means of combating cost-push inflation would depend upon the type of cost inflation presumed to exist as well as upon how the policy was administered. What follows, therefore, is an attempt at representative discussion of the anti-inflation value of the previously described national incomes policy in which consideration is given to the possibility that any of the several versions of cost inflation discussed in Chapter 3 might exist along with or in lieu of cost inflation theory No. 1 (i.e., wage-push inflation), which was treated in Part II of this book and thus will not be discussed again at this point.

Cost Inflation Theory No. 2—General Cost-Push. As observed in Chapter 3, one possible cost inflation theory, alternative to the wage-push idea, couches the analysis in very general terms—*i.e.,* where it is assumed that all prices (including the price of labor) rise at about the same rate.

A national incomes policy, if operated in anti wage-push ways, could be no more than partially effective as a means of counteracting this general cost inflation. The policy would be effective only insofar as inflationary pressures were the result of wage increases, and national incomes policy was an effective means of restraining these wage increases.

But wage increases are not the total explanation of general cost inflation; non-wage factor price movements also are relevant. Given general cost inflation and price stabilizing monetary and fiscal policy, national incomes policy, if administered in an optimum way, could be effective in equilibrating price-level stability and high employment. But it would be effective only to the degree that non wage-push inflation pressures were offset by a too low wage level. In other words, cost inflation could be suppressed by direct controls on wages, operated in non wage-push ways. This is unfortunate, for it is highly questionable if suppression of non wage-push inflation through government involvement in the wage administration task would result in a pattern of resource allocation any better than would occur in the absence of the policy. The cure seems no better than the disease.

National incomes policy would be much less effective when used to counteract general cost inflation, than when used to counteract one of the three forms of wage inflation. In addition to the problems which imperfect administration of the policy would bring, imposition of national incomes policy in a situation of this kind would require that workers suffer either the voluntary unemployment of general cost inflation, when suppressed by monetary and fiscal policy, or the inequitable wage which would be requisite for price-level stability and high employment.

Cost Inflation Theory No. 3—"Key" Cost-Push. A third category of inflation considered in Chapter 3 involves the assumption that certain costs are key costs in the inflation process. If the price of one of these key factors rises, so it is assumed, this increase will be communicated throughout the economy by means of a spiral or round effect.

As was explained in that chapter, this category of inflation theories encompasses a large number of sub-types of the cost inflation theory. A cost or price rise of almost any product or service, or group of products or services, could be the causal factor. For this reason it is necessary to know, specifically, what cost and price is assumed to be precipitating before the impact of a national incomes policy could be analyzed.

As demonstrated, the key cost could be wages in a particular sector of the economy, union determined wages, or even wages in general. If this be the case the reader is referred to Chapter 11 which deals with the wage inflation hypotheses.

Alternatively, if the key cost is anything other than wages or includes items other than wages, there would be some similarities between a national incomes policy program used in this instance and national incomes policy used as a means of counteracting general cost inflation. Government involvement in the wage administration task designed to help control these varieties of key cost inflation would require that workers suffer the discomforts and the inequities of federal involvement in the wage setting process, when workers were not wholly at fault for the inflationary experience, perhaps not even partially at fault. It would require, also, a wage administration program different from one which was solely anti wage-push.

The distinction between use of a national incomes policy program to combat general cost inflation and key cost-push inflation is that in the latter case the policy would not need to be applied to the entire economy. It could be applied, instead, to the offending sector only. Thus the standard of performance of national incomes policy would not need to be so great in this instance as in other situations where partial application of the policy was not a possibility.

Inequities in one sector of the economy, coming in part from failures of an incomes policy to yield an "ideal" pattern of wages, and in part from use of an incomes policy to combat inflation not of the wage-push type, could be balanced out against the national gains that would be realized if general inflation could be avoided. Of course, as explained in the chapter dealing with wage inflation hypotheses, this analysis would hold only so long as the inflationary round truly was caused by activities in one sector of the economy only. If the diagnosis of round inflation was incorrect, sector application of an incomes policy has the potential of causing severe misallocation of resources. Even so the policy might not halt the inflationary pressures.

National Incomes Policy and Cost Inflation. It is evident that the effectiveness of national incomes policy to combat cost inflation will depend in large part upon the type of cost inflation that exists, as well as upon whether the policy is anti wage-push in nature or is structured in some other way. National incomes policy to combat round inflation, particularly round inflation with a wage-push origin, could be effective. National incomes policy to combat general wage inflation or union wage inflation would have a number of disadvantages, particularly in the case of general wage inflation. National incomes policy to combat general cost inflation is least likely to be effective.

NATIONAL INCOMES POLICY AND STRUCTURALIST INFLATION

The final inflation explanation which will be considered is the structuralist thesis put forth by Charles L. Schultze.[2] Briefly, it is his contention that prices and wages tend to be more rigid downward than upward and that patterns of demand are in a continual state of flux. Under these conditions where demand is increasing, prices rise as do quantities supplied. By contrast, in those areas where demand is on the wane relatively, prices do not fall or fall slowly. According to this explanation, it is the combination of behavior in these two market situations that gives rise to some trend inflations.

Given the Schultze explanation of inflation cause, national incomes policy would have much the same impact as in the case of general cost inflation.

To the extent that the Schultze structuralist phenomenon was the result of downward wage rigidities, rather than non-wage rigidities, limits on wage bargaining would be effective as an anti-inflationary device, to the degree that they would be effective in dealing with any general wage inflation. Limits on wage bargaining are not going to be completely satisfactory as a means of controlling upward wage pressures of a general sort. Their introduction, given demand-cost inflation, would cause aberrations in patterns of resource allocation for this reason.

Downward wage rigidities also are not the total explanation for Schultze inflation. To the extent that it is the behavior of non-wage costs (prices) which cause Schultze structuralist type inflationary pressures, an incomes policy is not likely to be an effective counter measure. National incomes policy could be used to depress the level of wages so as to offset non-wage rigidities. But suppression of inflation in this case would have consequences similar to those that would result from suppression of any non-wage cost inflation. It is questionable if suppression of this kind of inflation by a too low wage level would result in a pattern of resource allocation any better than would result under any suppressed inflation. Again, imposition of the policy would require that workers suffer either the involuntary unemployment of cost inflation, when suppressed by

---

2. *Recent Inflation in the United States.*

monetary and fiscal policy, or the inequitable wage which would be the requisite of price-level stability and high employment. Selection of such a wage policy goal would require that policy makers know the type of inflation with which they were dealing, so that they could choose the proper wage policy objectives. It would require also that policy makers be able to cope with monetary and fiscal policy implications of any confusion in price-level signals that comes from attempting to implement price stabilizing monetary and fiscal policy while simultaneously attempting to handle some price-level fluctuation problems through wage policy adjustments.

The fact that Schultze considers wage and price rigidities the structural defect that leads to some trend inflations might imply an incomes policy just to introduce wage flexibility. This would be incorrect. A decision to control Schultze inflation via national incomes policy, combined with judicious use of monetary and fiscal policy, must take account of downward non-wage rigidities as well. If price-level stability and high employment are to be compatible objectives, national incomes policy must be used to restrict the total wage level, in addition to introducing wage flexibility. A restricted wage level would be necessary to offset downward price rigidities.

On the other hand, the Schultze hypothesis does suggest a possible means for simplifying the wage administration task that is not open in the case of general cost inflation. The appropriate remedy for Schultze inflation is downward wage and price flexibility in declining markets. Schultze inflation might be countered, therefore, by a program of selective controls directed only at declining markets. But there are problems inherent in a procedure of this kind.

Since markets experiencing declining demand are continually different, the industries covered by controls would have to shift from time to time. Also, in some markets it is more difficult to overcome non-wage rigidities by reducing the wage level than in others. For example, where wage cost is not a significant portion of total cost, wages may have to fall greatly before total costs fall. National incomes policy designed to overcome price rigidities may work severe hardship in some labor markets.

In addition the remote possibility does exist that manipulation of the level of wages, however extreme, will not cause prices to be any more responsive to changes in demand than previously. If this were the case, imposition of wage controls would mean that labor was forced to suffer control measures that were both restrictive and completely ineffective in accomplishing their primary task—that of introducing wage and *price* flexibility.

NATIONAL INCOMES POLICY IN NON WAGE-PUSH SITUATIONS

A rapid survey of national incomes policy operated in anti wage-push ways, but employed to combat non wage-push types of inflation, yields several conclusions.

A national incomes policy program designed primarily to counter wage-push inflation offers the greatest possibility of success when used to combat the type of inflation which it was designed to help control—wage-push inflation. The policy is by no means of equal value in all wage inflation situations, but in general it offers the greatest hope where inflation is of the wage-push type. National incomes policy offers some advantages when applied to other inflation situations, but in these instances the greatest value often comes when the policy is applied in non wage-push ways. Subject to the type of inflation with which the economy is faced, these methods would include: (1) efforts to promote general economic stability through less frequent wage change than presently exists, (2) efforts to repress general inflation through direct controls on wages only, and (3) efforts to limit only inflation due to wage behavior through an incomes policy, and to allow other cost-push pressures to continue and to continue to affect the general price-level.

National incomes policy, if operated in anti wage-push ways, relies heavily on private sources for market information. Consequently, the policy enjoys the strongest guarantees of success if those who supply the raw data are in sympathy with an incomes policy, both in principle and in practice. If those who supply the raw data oppose the wages authority, the incomes policy would be effective in accomplishing its goal only to the extent that the policy was adequately administered and enforced.

As demonstrated in Chapters 9, 10, and 11, adequate administration and enforcement is not beyond the realm of possibility. This is particularly the case where partial application of the policy is a possibility. To be administered and enforced adequately, the policy must result in a less ineffective pattern of resource allocation than would occur in its absence. This amounts to a requirement that the incomes policy adopted be less severe in its impact than the inflation or inflationary pressures that would exist in its absence. This result is entirely possible. It is less probable than the proponents of some sort of national incomes policy claim, but it is possible.

As demonstrated in Chapter 11, a national incomes policy program operated in anti wage-push ways, offers some chance of success when used to combat general wage inflation. It offers a greater chance of success when used to combat union inflation. This is particularly true if the policy can be directed against the unionized sector only. National incomes policy offers the greatest hope of all when used to control key wage-push inflation, provided the policy can be directed effectively against just the key sectors.

A national incomes policy program also could achieve some successes when used to combat demand inflation, general cost inflation, key cost inflation, or Schultze inflation. The results of application of an incomes policy in these four situations would not be equal. Moreover, it seems clear that, to be effective, the policy ought to be applied in non wage-push ways, and each situation would call for different variations in the policy.

Both the key cost-push and the Schultze hypotheses imply an incomes policy program that is limited to a sector of the economy only. The demand-pull and general cost-push hypotheses imply an incomes policy which is applied to the entire economy. But all four inflation theories imply a need for a policy program that does more than remove wage rigidities and neutralize excessive wage increases. With the exception of the demand-pull case, introduction of wage flexibility and prevention of excessive wage increases would ease the conflict between high employment and price-level stability. In the demand-pull case, elimination of pressures for excessive wage increases would add nothing since no such pressures are presumed to exist; whereas introduction of wage flexibility probably would complicate the task of the monetary and fiscal policy authorities rather than simplify it. But in none of the four cases would introduction of wage flexibility and removal of pressures for excessive wage increases be a complete answer to the postulated problems of inflation.

The establishment of a level and pattern of wages that was both appropriate and appropriately flexible would assist in the reduction of inflationary pressures only to the extent that inappropriate wage behavior was an inflation cause. In the instances just cited wage behavior was not the only reason for inflationary pressures. In all but the demand-pull case, non-wage cost-push forces also would be present. These cost-push forces undoubtedly could be offset by depressing the wage level, if wages were depressed far enough. Depressing the wage level also could assist in the control of demand inflation. But if inflationary pressures are restricted, in part, by placing restraint on the level of wages, two serious problems arise.

Reduction of inflationary pressures by restraining the level of wages would have an effect upon patterns of income distribution and upon patterns of resource allocation. The intensity of this impact would vary depending both upon the cause and upon the relative strength of the inflationary pressures to be contained. But some distortion would exist in every instance.

The proposition that non-wage cost inflation pressures should be offset by an incomes policy appears doubtful. Seemingly a superior approach would be to use the incomes policy only to control wage inflation, and not to attempt to use wage policy to correct non-wage problems, but administratively it might not be feasible to make a distinction of this kind. If not, a decision would have to be made as to whether the economic inequity of the too low wage level needed to neutralize inflationary pressures, partly non wage-push in origin, would be offset by the economic benefit of eliminating inflationary pressures. Alternatively, if it were possible to make a distinction between non-wage cost inflation and wage inflation, and to use the developed incomes policy to fight only the latter, a decision would have to be made as to whether wage inflation was a significant enough portion of total inflationary pressures to warrant imposition of a program so broad and far reaching.

If national incomes policy were used to fight non-wage inflation, in addition to the allocative effects that would result, reduction of inflationary pressures by restraining the level of wages also would complicate greatly the task of price stabilizing monetary and fiscal policy. Certainly, price-level increases can be repressed through direct controls. But price-level movements are the usual signal for monetary and fiscal policy action. Thus the question—is it wise to attempt to restrict price-level movements if they are the accepted guide to stabilization policy?

As a further problem, given repressed inflation, even the usual alternates to price-level movements as guides to stabilization policy will be distorted. Where repressed inflation exists, individual markets will be characterized by "scrambling," shortages, etc. The presence of these conditions thus becomes usual, rather than unusual, and the appropriateness of monetary and fiscal policy decisions taken, given repressed inflation, would hinge upon ability to determine when the symptoms of suppression were present to a greater (or lesser) extent than they should be.

In the course of the discussion in Chapter 3 the hope was expressed that it might be possible to develop a more universal inflation cure than methods currently employed. Certainly if such a cure could be developed its implementation would render less necessary current debates as to inflation cause.

Investigation indicates that a national incomes policy program could have some universal attributes for inflation control. Provided the policy was properly structured, it should be able to make a contribution to the control of any of the inflations, as classified according to cause, that were discussed in this study. But application of an incomes policy should be adjusted to suit the particular inflation experienced; and in some cases the form the policy ought to take is not certain.

Whenever there is general wage-push inflation, incomes policy ought to attempt to establish the level of wages most compatible with price-level stability continuously maintained. Even if it is union wage inflation or key wage-push inflation that is presumed to exist, instead of general wage-push inflation, the issue of structure of the policy does not get a great deal more complex. In these cases, the means of accomplishing the appropriate wage level may vary slightly in that the policy may be partial or general. But the objective still is clear. Any national incomes policy should be directed toward obtaining that level of wages most compatible with price-level stability.

When the task facing the wage authority is control of any inflation other than wage-push in type, not only may the incomes policy program used be either partial or general depending upon the situation, but the proper goal of the control program is in doubt. Should the incomes policy be employed just to prevent excessive increases in the wage level and to provide adequate flexibility in wages, or should the policy be used to suppress inflation not of the wage-push type?

If national incomes policy is to be used in non wage-push situations, several results can be expected depending upon the type of inflation experienced. Under certain conditions (demand inflation and many types of cost inflation) the impact of policy, if operated in anti wage-push ways,[3] could be slight—*i.e.*, no appreciable distortion in the level or pattern of wages. But the policy would not make much of a contribution of a positive nature either. Under other conditions (general cost inflation and certain varieties of round inflation), the impact of national incomes policy would be such as to enable at least partial control of price increases through some control of the wage bill.

But if an incomes policy is to be effective in controlling price-level increases not of the wage-push type, it should be directed towards the specific kind of inflation in existence. The policy should not be operated in anti wage-push ways. This is not possible unless and until (1) causes of particular inflationary experiences can be diagnosed with greater accuracy, and (2) the appropriate goal of the incomes policy, in each case, can be determined with more certainty.

The above conclusions take on even greater significance when the fact is considered that the various theories as to inflation cause actually are attempts to isolate a significant inflation cause or one that is significant some of the time. This is particularly true of the cost inflation theories, as they assume the possibility of demand inflation some of the time.

In the real world there is evidence to indicate that inflations are not uniquely caused over a period of time or at one time. If this is so, it can be expected that national incomes policy as an anti-inflationary device would have two important effects in varying degrees: (1) aberrations in the pattern and level of wages and (2) some inflation control effect.

3. National incomes policy operated in such a way that the wage level selected is that most compatible with high level full employment, given price stabilizing monetary and fiscal policy.

INDEX